THE SEEDS OF
CHILDHOOD

THE SEEDS OF CHILDHOOD

A Psycho-Spiritual Parenting Guide

Phyllis Hampton

To order additional copies of this book, contact:
Xlibris Corporation
1-888-795-4274
www.Xlibris.com
Orders@Xlibris.com
39044

CONTENTS

CONTENTS

INTRODUCTION

The Seeds of Childhood addresses beliefs and concepts that we, as adults and as a society, perhaps quite unconsciously, instill in the extremely fertile minds of children. We plant these "seeds" in a child's belief system that the child innocently accepts as *truth*[1] solely because we say they are so.

Parents are their children's first teachers and most powerful influences. Whether the seeds parents establish in their child's mind are beneficial or detrimental, these seeds form the very foundation of a youngster's reality. The parents' beliefs and concepts largely make up the subconscious blueprint that will direct the life of their son or daughter.

The seeds instilled by adults command a strong positive or negative impact over the quality of an individual's unfolding life experience. Many of these beliefs and assumptions are passed in societies and families from generation to generation, like priceless heirlooms, but often with little thought as to their validity and psycho-spiritual consequences.

Traditional childhood conditioning provides children with concrete definitions of right and wrong and can give them a road map of directives to achieve common goals. Rules of behavior and steps to success are neatly laid out. To reap the benefits of this antiquated indoctrination, an adherent to this system blindly follows the rules without deviation and never doubts their validity or truthfulness. Such ritualistic systems of managing life have a common major flaw, however; they rarely take into account the individualism and spirits of children.

---

[1] True—When I use the word *true* by itself or as the root of another, I am referring to that which conforms in essence with the natural or universal laws of consciousness and energy. I believe that when we speak in such phrases as, "My truth is . . ." or, "That is your truth . . ." when we actually mean, "I believe that . . ." we corrode the pure meaning of the word.

Therefore, a revised paradigm of parenting, nurturing and teaching is needed so that children's images of themselves and their world develop more naturally by empirical and objective means. Children then have the necessary climate to discover their innate selves rather than trying to fit inflexible specifications outlining how and what they should be.

Every child is unique and possesses an individual *emotional makeup*,[2] *spiritual identity*[3] *and life mission*.[4] When any child's development into his greatest potential is not inhibited in any way, not only are the natural abilities of the child not limited, but humanity gains in the very renewing and regenerating process innate within our species.

Many parents today are aware that parenting and teaching styles used by their parents and teachers, and taught by the experts of the past, are not working with their children. These philosophies primarily relied on molding the child into a *perfect child*.[5] Out of an innate sense of self-preservation, children often react defensively to being included in this confining and unhealthy hierarchy. For example, behavioral syndromes and learning disorders such as Attention Deficit Disorder (ADD) and Attention Deficit/Hyperactive Disorder (ADHD) are prevalent in our children. Traditional pedagogy based largely on mass behavior modification is no longer an effective approach to development of well-adjusted, happy children.

The most significant consequence of inflexible traditional conditioning is the arresting of the creative and innovative faculty of the mind. Several adults who were conformists as children now face the largest decision of their lives—either to continue living unfulfilling materialistic lives, or to face the fact that something essential is missing. In my counseling work, I have met a few brave souls who chose to define and address the emptiness in their lives by exploring new perspectives and directions. Starting over at any age is a daunting task, but those who persevere in searching for a new road that is more natural for them tap into the delight of knowing who they

---

[2]   Our emotional makeup pertains to how we have interpreted our life to the present moment. This history plays a large part in how we will interpret and be affected by our lives both now and in the future.

[3]   Our spiritual identity is who we are innately. It refers to the individuality of our soul.

[4]   Our life mission refers to the collective of what we are to experience, accomplish and understand in order for our soul to awaken and evolve.

[5]   A perfect child is one that meets the criteria to rank in a hierarchy of achievement. There is no such child as a perfect one, although some parents strive unsuccessfully and blindly to create one. This especially happens to a first-born.

are underneath all of their old rules and regulations. Natural seeds can be kept dormant by denial of their existence, but they will develop into their magnificence when nurtured.

Whatever possible should be done in children's early years to foster a more natural evolution and nurture their individuality. In this way, later massive restructuring of their lives will be unnecessary, as it is for many adults.

There are children today who are breaking from old models; extremely bright, talented and creative children among them. Slowly, the old methods of child nurturing are being challenged by creative and dedicated individuals whose focus is to help children grow and evolve into their unique and individual selves. Mothers and fathers are among these ranks.

In many cases, parents are asked to change their beliefs about parenting and their parenting styles. Change is difficult, but parents can, and do, modify their habits and beliefs frequently. Why? Because they deeply love their children and families, and they take risks for their benefit. The parent/young child bond remains the strongest from outside influence because of the sense of responsibility and deep love felt by most parents toward their children. When the bond between parent and child is strong, a parent is able to positively change and the entire family structure participates in that transformation.

Though I observe the parent/child relationship occasionally falter in the mainstream of society, I also see many mothers and fathers who are reigniting this strong bond, rekindling the desire to adopt a more soul-nurturing parenting philosophy.

I am a daughter, a mother and now a grandmother. I struggled with many issues as a child, and I address several of them in this book to parents. As I explored psychology and then psycho-spiritual studies, I searched for different parenting beliefs and methods that could have enriched my life and the life of my daughter. As my explorations progressed, I visited many repressed misunderstandings and wounds of childhood that surfaced. It was then possible for me to reframe and heal them. My healing work is ongoing, and each successful resolution rewards me with greater freedom from my unconscious past and its fears and misconceptions.

The Seeds of Childhood goes beyond the standard parenting book. It presents valuable ideas to mothers and fathers to nurture the spirits of their children. It explains how parents can help their sons and daughters be aware of and manage their emotions. This book also offers suggestions to help aid children to develop sound decision-making skills. Many excellent books are available that discuss the physical development of children and how to prepare them for the physical world. There are few instructional works, however, which help parents lay groundwork for children to greet life with emotional and mental composure and flexibility.

Because my work with my past childhood has been so positive in shaping my current happiness, I invite parents to also consider their own childhood experiences as they read the book. I give examples throughout to facilitate these reflections.

With this book, I seek to bring clarity to the uniqueness of children so their childhood journey is one of natural growth and development. In addition, I offer a simple system that hopefully will trigger new insights for parents about their children and their own childhoods. My desire is that my suggestions bring freshness to the field of parenting so our children will develop into healthy, whole and fulfilled human beings.

FROM THE SEED . . . THAT'S ME

Total Confidence
       of what I am . . .
   makes Me the Lion
         and the Lamb.

While the God I am to be
      is grown from Seed that is but Me.

The Me . . .
     who creates by Effort and Will
        The Greatness that is . . .
           by being still.

By listening . . .
      to the Voice of Soul
         that fashions Parts . . .
            into One Whole.

And by Confidence of Knowing
    that within each Life
    I can only grow
    and create this Me
       By meeting Strife.

To slowly grow . . .
    to slowly be . . .
       A God in Greatness
         from the Seed . . .
           that's Me.

:From the Poems of Gerardus

CHAPTER 1

The Fertile Soil of a Child's Mind

Children have an intrinsic, essential, but greatly unrecognized intelligence beyond what is committed to memory and stored facts. Children seem to drink up information about their environment, which leads to a common misconception that a *child*[1] is a relatively "deaf and dumb" creature who comes into life on a blank slate.

Humans, and indeed all living things, have an innate wisdom that is quite remarkable. They ultimately are destined to blossom into who and what they naturally are. Let us compare a human to a rose. How does a rose know to be a rose and not a sunflower? More importantly, how does it know to be a red one instead of a white one? Within the class of roses, there are numerous different types having very different qualities. Even within the same species, roses will display unique characteristics. Even as roses share many similarities as a botanical classification, each is distinctive. When nurtured, each rose will bloom according to its own inner essence.

We humans share similar physical features, such as two legs, two arms, two eyes, a mouth, bones, blood, muscles, and a brain. But each of us is set apart from others by seemingly infinite variations. The fact that each fingerprint is matchless is a good physical example of our distinctive makeup.

Our inner natures which include our potentials, talents, personalities, and temperaments, are also distinctive and are not decided by direct parental and societal programming. Our individual *essences*[2] are far greater than the results

---

[1] A child (healthy psycho-spiritually) is a being incarnate who has not yet mastered the potential skills and knowledge necessary to successfully inhabit his or her physical and social environment.

[2] The essence of something or someone is its unchanging, intrinsic nature in its most pure form.

of learned behavior. Although our innate characteristics may not be obvious in our routine lives, they are the foundation of our individuality beyond our identification with our programmed *characters and body costumes*.[3] Although childhood programming and conditioning can slow our development into our greatest selves, our inner natures will always push us to express who we essentially are.

Since the 1950s, science has been aware of DNA encoding stored in the double helix strands contained in every cell of our bodies. The study of DNA reveals correspondences to individual physical traits, potentials, and even diseases. Hard sciences continue to develop vast knowledge about our physical bodies. But what about individual traits and qualities that cannot be perceived by the physical senses? Perhaps there are codes that equally define our unique talents, our general dispositions, and even the special circumstances into which we are born. Although these markers cannot yet be determined by scientific means, they are the components that give rise to the enigmatical paradoxes that make us different and diverse.

Even at birth, for instance, siblings born to the same parents may be very different in temperament. Music may calm one child, while the other might react to it as an irritant. These reactions are the result of different inherent personalities. Even though these indications are rudimentary in infancy, they are perceptible enough for us to recognize that every child is distinctive.

Each child possesses an innate "recipe" of individuality, born with individual potentials that are the result of his/her unique *destiny*[4] and his/her *evolutionary history*.[5] These seeds are pre-planted by our unique

---

[3] An individual's character and body costume is one's physical expression at any given time. We often believe that this expression, the one we know in this lifetime, is the only one we ever had. Our essences, however, have had many characters and bodies throughout its evolution. It is quite likely it will have many more.

[4] The assumption is made in this writing that each of us has a mission—an individual evolutionary agenda—that our Soul, or Authentic Self, has defined to complete or gain in accomplishment with regard to the current lifetime. There is great joy and anticipation when we discover our destiny and begin to focus on its actualization.

[5] Evolutionary history is based upon the belief that the Soul is currently utilizing several lifetimes to complete its process to return to The Oneness with God, The Creator, The One, The Universe, The All That Is, or whatever title an individual prefers. The experiences, wisdom and knowledge garnered to this end make up the Soul's evolutionary history.

destiny and past *incarnational*[6] history, and will germinate in some way within the fabric of our lives.

If we study the biographies and autobiographies of extraordinary human achievers, we can understand this principle more easily. Dr. Albert Einstein's life exemplifies both individual destiny and evolutionary history within a lifetime. His destiny included uncovering, understanding and creating a mathematical and scientific language that laid a foundation for others to study the universe more extensively. In all probability, his evolutionary history would reveal lifetimes dedicated to this mission in one way or another. This continual focus then culminated in his phenomenal recent lifetime with which we are familiar.

It is hard to imagine that anything would have stopped Einstein from dedicating his life to this mission. Hypothetically, it is doubtful that he would have settled for being an actor, a general in the armed forces, or anyone other than whom he was destined to be.

Although most of us are not presently experiencing such an exceptional lifetime as Einstein's, we all are working toward the culmination of our Souls' ultimate fate. Einstein's exemplary focus and perseverance is a remarkable model to emulate in overcoming whatever distractions and limitations occur in the unfolding of our individual paths.

While there are underlying *potentials*[7] and qualities in every child, it is also important to understand the developing child in psychological terms of

---

[6]   There are many forms of belief regarding reincarnation, but a basic and fundamental principle underlying all of the various philosophies and schools is this (as paraphrased from W. W. Atkinson, *Reincarnation and The Law of Karma*; Yogi Publication Society: 1938, p. 8): There is, in man, an "immaterial Something" called Soul, Spirit, Inner Self, etc., which does not perish at the death or disintegration of the body, but which continues as an entity. This entity, after an interval of rest and possible reflection, is re-born into a new infant body and proceeds to live a new life in the new body, more or less unconscious of its past existences. Even though largely unconscious of past life experiences, the being contains within itself the "essence" or results of its past lives. These past experiences go to make up its new character or personality.

[7]   The collective and unique individual capacities and innate qualities we are born with. Potentials are key elements in the unfoldment of our destinies and in our ongoing spiritual evolution.

the *mind.*[8] **The mind of a child is like fertile soil. Seeds (beliefs) can be planted which impact the emergence and unfolding of the unique being of that child.** These beliefs define an individual's unique perception of his/her reality, or what he/she thinks is true. For instance, if a person is led to believe that her musical ability is not as good as someone's intellectual talents, there is a good chance that she will abandon the effort it will take to develop that musical ability. She might compete in the intellectual arena and even become proficient in book knowledge. However, happiness, joy and the love of what she does are often missing.

The metaphor of a threaded loom may help clarify the forces that influence a developing child. In this vision, the vertical threads on a child's loom are the potentials at birth. These signify his/her inherent state of being. One thread may be a potent musical talent; another may be an urge to understand and deeply feel compassion. Still another may be a karmic thread to deal with and heal resentment with another being. The vertical threads are relatively fixed. They reveal themselves through urges, desires, dreams, and synchronicities in life.

The lateral threads of our metaphorical loom are woven "by hand" in this lifetime. They are the tools the child develops, the beliefs he/she acquires, his/her feelings, and the choices he/she makes. The lateral threads are what we usually think of as the individual. They are, however, only a person's physical expression, or character, as opposed to his/her essential potentials.

The weaving of our lateral, physical threads, and our vertical, metaphysical threads creates the mystery of who we are. When we are conscious of both, we develop the physical, psychological and social tools to creatively express our greatest selves and complete our unique destinies.

Parents begin influencing the weaving of their child's lateral threads and the planting of seeds at the child's conception. If these threads and seeds are positive, nurturing, empowering, truthful and helpful ones, the child has a head start on the creation and completion of a beautiful life tapestry.

Imagine if parents, teachers and others capable of influencing the minds and hearts of children were aware of the presence of these vertical threads. What a potentially powerful impact these resources and models would have

---

[8]   The mind is the imperceptible component of our being that accumulates assumed facts, memories, and our beliefs about ourselves, others, and our environment. It is the component that is frequently thought of as our consciousness and the faculty of thinking, reasoning and applying knowledge. The mind's physical instrument is the brain.

on the weavings of the lives of children, helping them assemble life tools and develop the qualities that would assist them.

Children who receive such guidance cultivate *confidence,*[9] which lights their way to living thriving and flourishing lives. The next chapter focuses on the concept of confidence and how children can develop this priceless quality.

---

[9] Throughout this book, confidence refers *to ". . . the expression of your essential, authentic, primal self . . . [the inner state of mind] that you are capable and lovable."* Quote from the teachings of Jerhoam, an enlightened teacher. (More information may be obtained through website *www.Jerhoam.com*.) You express confidence when you express who you innately are.

CHAPTER 2

Confidence

If we explore the deep meaning of our chapter title, we can assert that **confidence is the state of knowing who you essentially are.** Confident individuals radiate inner assuredness and contentment with life and with themselves. Confidence differs from *arrogance.*[1] Confidence does not depend upon being better than another, being more highly thought of than another, or asserting yourself as a way to gain rewards and confirmations for your efforts. A confident person is not concerned with outward appearances or validation, but is instead looking inward to know themselves and creating this awareness in physical reality.

How do parents foster confidence in their children? The answer is simple: Nurture their essential spirits. One way for moms and dads to do this is to remind their youngsters periodically that they are here to discover, to learn, to gain self-knowledge, and ultimately to be of service in the world. These important seeds automatically incubate their fundamental talents and aptitudes. Their destinies and inner potentials begin to sprout from the roots of their own genuine identity.

Parents can also assist their sons and daughters to practice the process of finishing what they desire to complete. A sizable ingredient of confidence is the inner knowing that one is able to practically manage both himself/herself and the world to succeed in chosen undertakings. As children repeatedly practice this, they concurrently develop responsibility, patience and perseverance, three character traits crucial to support confidence.

---

[1] An arrogant person seems convinced of his/her own importance. Arrogance often originates from an attempt to assuage a deep inner sense of inferiority and/or self-doubt.

When a child of any age has an idea to do something—tackle a task, master a game or skill—a parent is presented with an ideal opportunity to help the child practice successful completion. If a 7-year-old girl wants to write a letter to her grandmother, her mom or dad can help her focus on what she would like to say to her grandmother, assist with spelling, and help ready the letter to post. Their daughter not only practices her writing, spelling, and cognitive skills, she develops the inner knowing that she can accomplish a task that she chooses to do. She also gains experience in gathering the elements and assistance needed to successfully complete her undertaking.

If a 10-year-old boy loves music and wants to learn to play the piano, an ongoing opportunity opens for his parents to assist him in understanding and developing commitment to a goal. Their son agrees to go to piano lessons and commits to the daily practice required to reach his objective. The boy will have the chance to explore patience, perseverance and responsibility.

It is wise for parents to set a time frame to revisit the relative long-term commitments their sons and daughters make. As life gets more complex with age, so do the elements of successful parenting. Long-term commitments differ from short-term tasks in that they carry many unknown and variable factors. A child should not be locked into a pledge forever that does not serve him/her. Instead of being passionate about learning to play the piano, perhaps the boy in the above example saw it as a way to be accepted by the little girl next door who takes lessons. His parents can assist their son in being clear about what his true wishes are.

If, however, the boy pledged to take piano lessons for six months, and two months into the regimen he decides, for whatever reason, he would like to stop, his parents can compassionately assist him in learning about commitment. Unless studying piano is a terrible fit for their son, it might serve his greater development to assist him to keep his six-month commitment. He may find that studying piano suits him after all, or he may not. It really doesn't matter because he learned about commitment, patience, and self-knowledge.

These types of experiences facilitate a child in gaining awareness of him/herself. They also are important situations that can aid a child's emotional and ethical growth and development.

Some parents teach these lessons by holding their child to a commitment no matter what. I've heard some parents say such things as, "I knew you would never stick with it! You wanted to play the piano—now get in there and practice!" The child might learn about "sticking with it," but it is likely he will not venture out and commit to another desire easily. The price is too great. His inner confidence is shaken. Parents who instead talk with their children about the larger lessons and significance inherent in such experiences help them develop the resources necessary to confidently manage their lives.

Children radiate confidence when they are being themselves. Wise parents can nurture their children's essential identity and assist them to develop helpful values, tools and skills. It *is* possible for children to keep their inner flame alive as they go into the world as young adults, living confidently a fulfilling life congruent with who intrinsically are.

The next chapter is devoted to creativity, another important ability for parents to foster and nurture in children.

CHAPTER 3

The Elixir of Creativity

The most powerful ability children can develop in their early years to serve them in later life is *creativity.*[1] It is an *elixir*[2] because it brings continued freshness, growth and renewal. Most children are instinctively creative. In observing their uninhibited play, you can watch them use the most unorthodox props. For children, the joy is in creative play instead of the outcome. This is the essence of creativity.

Creativity unfolds throughout the stages of childhood. Very young children, up to the age of 3 to 4, are not overtly creative. They are busy learning and familiarizing themselves with the physical tools of life—the whats and hows of their physical bodies and environment. The responsibility of wise parents at this stage is to teach their young child about the delights and dangers of the physical world and of the consequences of his/her interaction with it. The tightrope walked by parents throughout all stages, but especially when their sons and daughters are very young, is that of keeping their vulnerable children safe without suppressing their growing interest and mastery of their environment.

As children mature into pre-school age, they begin to add social themes to their exploration. Creativity becomes apparent at this time. Pre-schoolers are

---

[1]   Creativity is the ability to think "outside the box." It is the foundation of original thought, invention, and problem solving. *"Creativity is inventing, growing, taking risks, breaking rules, making mistakes, and having fun."* Quote: Mary Lou Cook.

[2]   An elixir, metaphorically, refers to a magical type of element or agent that changes negativity (denseness) into positivism (light). In alchemy, an elixir is thought of as a magical or medicinal potion that transforms base metals into gold. In the spiritual sense, it is a magical agent that offers eternal or everlasting life.

equally as open to the exploration of feelings and psycho-social environment as they are to their physical world. They and their playmates may begin to make believe and assume various characters in their play. Children who are full of life delight in experimenting with all kinds of characters, themes and relationships.

At this point the parents' judgment that a character or theme the child might be imitating or creating is "good or bad" or "right or wrong" can have an effect on the child. Some parents fear that because their child plays the "bad guy" in his little drama, it means he is headed to a life of crime. When a little boy is playing Luke Skywalker and another is playing Darth Vader, the modern good guy/bad guy archetypes, the boys see it only as pretend. They are using the different roles to accustom themselves to how actions and reactions work, and to become familiar with prevalent social themes and myths. To them the acting out of these is play in purest form.

In 1956, the noted psychiatrist, *Erik Erikson,*[3] developed his "Eight Stages of Development," of social and emotional development of children and teenagers. Through wide-ranging experience in psychotherapy, including extensive experience with children and adolescents, Erikson regarded each stage as a "psychosocial crisis," which demands resolution before the next stage can be satisfactorily negotiated.

Erikson's stage theory provides the basis for many child social-emotional development models. The first stage Erikson describes is "Learning Basic Trust Versus Basic Mistrust," (from infancy through the first one or two years of life). The second stage is "Learning Autonomy versus Shame," (between about 18 months-2 years of age, through 3 ½ to 4 years of age). Erikson's third stage is "Learning Initiative Versus Guilt," (from about 3 1/2 years of age to the entry into formal school). This stage is crucial in the development of creativity. During the "play age," as Erikson calls it, the healthily developing child learns: To imagine, to broaden his skills through play of all sorts, including fantasy; to cooperate with others; to lead as well as to follow. Erikson goes on to observe that when immobilized by guilt, the child is: Fearful; hangs on the fringes of groups; continues to depend unduly on adults; and is restricted both in the development of play skills and in imagination.

As long as children's play is safe during the third stage described above, allow them to imagine and pretend freely. **There is a time in childhood**

---

[3]   Eric Erikson (1902-1994) is known world-wide as teacher, clinician and theorist in the area of human development. Additional information on the Eight Stages of Development and ego development can be found in Erikson's book: (1994), *Identity and the Life Cycle.* New York: Norton Press.

development to teach critical discernment, but generally, before the ages of 6 to 8, judgments only serve to inhibit exploration and creativity.

Parents are expected by society to teach children socially acceptable behavior, which often includes popular and trendy social standards for child development and behavior that are not based on natural childhood patterns. Children up to the ages of 6 are unable to understand and assimilate the concept of right and wrong. Because they are naturally self-absorbed, they perceive everything to be about them personally. A parent might say, "Don't do that—that is bad." What their child might hear and subsequently feel is, "Don't do that, you are bad."

In the natural development of children, the period between ages of 4 to 8 is a fertile time to plant the seeds of cooperation rather than separation. Let's look again at the example of the two little boys playing the "good guy" and the "bad guy." This is an opportunity for the boys to creatively work out differences. Perhaps the hero and the villain will work together in figuring out how to procure an extra snack, or to finagle another hour of play time together! Adults can foster cooperative effort, or teach judgment and separation.

Another example: Consider two little girls playing dress-up. Creativity flows as they try on grown-up clothes and compose most delightful dialogues. This does not threaten many parents. However, if one of the little girls dresses up as and acts somewhat provocatively, parents are concerned. It is likely that adults fear that the girl is on the road to self-destruction and something must immediately be done to save her.

Unless sexually abused, little girls merely act out what they see on TV. At their young ages, they cannot distinguish making themselves attractive (perhaps as Mom or Auntie may do), and dressing seductively. If the play is of a transient nature, it is wise to let it blow over. The bigger the deal made out of something relatively harmless, the more likely it will cause confusion.

Two helpful phrases for parents to use with their children are: "What are you playing now?" and "Tell me about it." When parents use these phrases, children have an opportunity to explain what they are thinking. As adults, we often assume what is going on with them and react on those assumptions. Often these assumptions are inaccurate. This can be hurtful to a child's sense of significance. **It takes relatively few times of discounting his/her fragile perceptions before self-doubt and withdrawal become apparent in a child's thinking and behavior.**

Early childhood is the stage of human development when creativity blossoms, if protected and wisely guided. **When parents permit their children spontaneous creative play they nurture imaginative and original**

thinkers. Conversely, when children's creativity is stunted, it has deep, dispiriting effects upon the evolution of their talents and innate qualities. Allow children to innocently play and imagine without assuming they will become the characters they are imagining to be. Allow children to create and become familiar with various life roles and themes.

As creative children mature, they trust themselves to resourcefully meet challenges and solve problems. When wisely guided, children find ways to imaginatively express joy and cooperation.

Many *adults,*[4] conversely, are stuck in a rut of behavior. They begin each day in the same way, eat the same foods, see the same people, do the same work and think the same thoughts. Habitual living is usually a direct or indirect result of creativity hindered by the development of fear during the early childhood years. Somewhere in their childhoods, these individuals develop a fear of expressing themselves creatively. In their minds, they come to believe that creativity and safety are incompatible. Many mothers and fathers may have succumbed to this fear to develop and express their creativity. Parenting offers them the opportunity for them to go beyond what they learned as children, to be open and to learn along with their children.

---

[4] A healthy adult is a being incarnate who has mastered skills and knowledge to a sufficient degree to interact successfully with his/her physical and social environment.

CHAPTER 4

The Parent as Teacher

Parents are their sons and daughters first teachers. Mothers and fathers teach children about their world and how to safely interact with it. Many of parents' early lessons are practical in nature, such as tying a shoe, eating healthy meals, crossing the street safely, and staying with a responsible adult.

When parents do not know what role to assume toward their children, confusion for both the parents and their children often results. An aware parent realizes and relates this attitude to his/her child, "I can be friendly, but right now I cannot be a friend like that little friend of yours. As your parent, I am a nurturer. But, most importantly, I am your first teacher."

As their child's first teachers, parents must stay objective and composed as much as possible. A parent can go so far as to tell their child, "I'm here to supervise your education. You are born from the universe. The universe reasoned I am the best teacher for you, and this is what I know. Anything else that I do not know, you'll have to get later, but this is what I *do* know."

In addition to practical knowledge and skills that parents must teach to help their children integrate into society, they can also educate and share basic technical and practical knowledge with their sons and daughters. For instance, a father who works as a plumber can teach his interested son or daughter about the skills and principles of plumbing. A physician mother can teach her child about the body and about health and illness. A parent who knows computers and shares that knowledge with his/her child lays an important building block in that child's foundational learning and expertise.

Psychologically, children with teaching parents know what to expect from the most important people in their lives. They are practically prepared for adulthood; and consistency in the parent-as-teacher role lays a valuable framework that can stabilize the often rocky relationship periods of adolescence and early adulthood.

Adopting the role of a nurturing teacher has significant subtle benefits as well. For instance, when you help your child overcome a difficult homework assignment, assisting him/her to discover the patience, resourcefulness and self-discipline necessary to complete the assignment, you participate in your son's or daughter's sense of accomplishment. Your shared experience often transcends words, inspiriting and inspiring both of you.

Childhood is the time for children to explore their unique selves and learn about the world they live in. It is the time to develop the skills to help them confidently enter into society. As they mature, children must learn the intricacies of our conversational language and embark on studies that will serve them in their lives and later work. It is equally important that they learn about the environment and their society, with all of its troubles and blessings. Children need their parents' knowledge, wisdom, support and understanding to help them interact with their world in an empowered and healthy way.

How parents reflexively and consciously teach what they know to their children is defined as their parenting style and is central to how their children receive and make use of the instruction. The next chapter will review a few reflexive parenting styles and will focus on how parents can become more conscious in their methods.

CHAPTER 5

Parenting Styles

As parents commit to becoming their child's first teachers, their *parenting styles*[1] consequently become those based on educating and guiding. Most of us have had experiences with teachers who instinctively knew how to make learning fun and how to nurture our budding spirits and deep sense of selves with an appropriate mix of discipline, creativity and acceptance. I would highly recommend emulating these teaching qualities with your children. This is challenging for many of us because we have not learned about parenting styles and their significance, either by standard instruction or by them consciously being modeled by our own parents.

As we have children, we usually tend either to model or choose not to raise our families the way our parents raised us. For example, a mother of two small children said that she knew only two ways to respond toward her children: To either react in the way her parents had habitually reacted toward her and her siblings, or to do exactly the opposite. Most parents raise their sons and daughters to the best of their abilities with great love and devotion. However, unintentionally they might be inclined toward being overly-authoritative, overly-permissive, overly-protective, or overly-detached or absent. Anything "overly" is extreme to a fault, and encumbers the parent-as-teacher role.

Effective and wise parenting involves being flexible, objective and protective in our day-to-day dealings with our children. When we become mindful of how we parent, we make conscious choices in our parenting approaches that will support our children's utmost psycho-spiritual, psycho-social and physical development.

---

[1] A parenting style is a parent's most consistent way of responding or reacting toward his/her child.

Most of us have seen extreme parenting styles. They are everywhere: In the grocery store, at the ball field, at a parent-teacher conference. These parenting models are symptomatic of an underlying unease and misunderstanding of the fundamental nature of children and their collective and individual maturation processes. All of the "overly" parenting methods affect a child's self-identification, confidence and development of healthy boundaries.

Overly-authoritative parents believe that they must make almost every decision for their children. These parents interpret any opposing thought, expression or decision by their children as improper and therefore must be reformed. Such dominating parents are often fearful that they will lose control and their imaginative and uninhibited children are becoming "willful." Authoritative parents commonly believe in the "perfect child" standard, tending to overly-discipline and overly-correct the behavior and thinking of their son or daughter. They feel they must shape him/her to a pre-determined standard rather than responding to the child's fundamental nature and maturity level.

One outstanding characteristic of overly-authoritarian parents is the hesitation to allow children to make their own decisions. **It is important for parents, as their children's first teachers, to _promote_ decision-making when it does not threaten the safety of the child or others.** This gives children the protective freedom to take baby steps in openly expressing and experimenting with their current subjective situations. If a 3-year-old girl wants to wear only pink clothes, she is making a choice that hurts no one. Three or 4-year-olds are able to select from their closets what color or what outfit to wear. Children of 5 or 6 will have the potential to occasionally choose the type of foods in each food group they prefer and which playmates they favor. Seven or 8-year-olds usually are able to choose from a few suitable extra-curricular activities.

Teaching mothers and fathers provide their children with safe but flexible parameters, allowing them to make decisions and live with the consequences of their decisions. They are helping their youngsters cultivate confidence to make appropriate choices now, which will evolve into their making healthy choices as adults. Parents who understand the various stages of psycho-spiritual child development define appropriate boundaries that adapt as their children mature.

Another type of "overly" parental style is overly-permissive, the other extreme of overly-authoritarian. **Overly-permissive parents often fail to set appropriate boundaries. As a consequence, their children often are**

deluged by life without the safety of parental limit-setting and the benefit of their parents' crucial insight and guidance.

An example of overly-permissive parenting might be the following: A child of 10 decides that he wants to change schools because he is angry or hurt by something his teacher has done. An overly-permissive parent probably would not go so far as to allow the child to change schools. However he/she might react over-sympathetically, sharing in the child's reaction before totally understanding the situation. Parents, as their child's first teacher, will be able to sort out what transpired at school and handle the situation beneficially for all concerned. If this essential step is skipped, a habit of reaction—as opposed to working through difficulties—is frequently planted in the child. The child will learn the role of *victim*.[2]

In the above instance, a teaching, guiding parent can provide the opportunity for the child to talk about and observe his reality, his assumptions about his reality, and how he interacts with it. The boy also has assistance in thinking through consequences rather than having to suffer them. Perhaps most importantly, the boy gains the valuable skills and practical experience to handle difficult or adverse situations throughout his life.

Reasonable, age-appropriate and consistent boundaries offer children the necessary safety they need to feel secure in their formative years. Metaphorically, children are provided the opportunity to learn to float in friendly waters before they tackle swimming in the ocean of the greater society. As a result, children who have been nurtured in this way are more likely to break down problems and challenges in order to successfully manage them. They grow up able to master life instead of being at its mercy.

Two other parenting styles are the absent or overly-detached parent and the overly-protective parent. These two "overly" parenting styles perhaps are easier to distinguish than the authoritarian and permissive styles because their effects on children are usually more apparent.

When parents are frequently physically or emotionally absent, children can be either chronically angry or excessively compliant. For instance, parents who are addicted to any substance or behavior are often detached from parenting their children. The bulk of the adults' attention often goes to placating their addiction rather than being aware of and meeting the needs of their youngsters. Frequently parents who are preoccupied, such as going

---

[2]   A victim is a role that is played by individuals when they do not know their power to change a negative situation. For them, someone or something else is responsible for whatever unpleasantness they feel.

through a terrible divorce or working 18 hours a day also are often detached and emotionally absent. There is little time or energy to effectively parent.

Children of absent or overly-detached parents often react with thoughts of, "It doesn't matter that my parents aren't here for me," and/or "What did I do that is so horrible that my parents don't want to be with me?" In the first case, children's pain is so intense that they will make excuses for their parents. They may try to prove themselves above needing the parental nurturing and attention that all children require. In the second case, children will search for different ways to be and act in order to please their parents so they will want to be with them.

Of all "overly" parenting styles, the absent or overly-detached one can be the most devastating to children. Great amounts of a child's energy must be expended in trying to gain the love and acceptance of the parent or coming to terms with a bleak reality of disconnection with his/her mother or father. Often this task seems insurmountable, and the child's only recourse is to deny the problem or declare him or herself as unlovable.

Opposite of absent or overly-detached parents are those who are overprotective. **Because of great anxiety, overly-protective parents do not allow their children to face adversity or take part in any unstructured situation for fear the child will meet harm, defeat or unpleasantness.** Many of these adults interpret extreme concern and worry about their children as loving behavior. Often this belief is based on a fear, either conscious or *subconscious,*[3] that the child will not be safe unless the parent has tight control of all situations. Anxiety-ridden parents take their responsibility so seriously that it is suffocating for their children.

An anxious mother may worry about the potential abduction of her 6-year-old daughter; she might deny her the freedom to walk alone in their quiet neighborhood to visit a friend just four houses away. Another might worry about her son's physical well-being to a point that he develops chronic anxiety about his state of health. It is one thing to be cautious and aware of dangers not understood by your child. It is another, however, to allow worry to escalate to such a degree that the child is fearful of natural exploration. Appropriate trust suffers.

We teach children anxiety and fear, often without being conscious of what we are doing. These potent seeds, subconsciously planted, inhibit children

---

[3] The subconscious is the part of the mind that contains assumptions, data and programming which one is not fully aware of, but that has a profound controlling influence upon their actions and feelings.

from developing the wise courage needed to discover who they are and what their identity is in the world.

Those who have childhood experiences with "overly" parenting styles often experience: Lack of self-assurance in their own reasoning and decision making ability; development of resentment toward parents and other authority figures because of feeling essentially inadequate, untrustworthy, or incapable; increasing need to rely on others to make decisions that directly affect them. When we, as parents, are aware of our tendencies to be overly authoritative, permissive, detached, or protective, we have the opportunity to break old reflexive habits that serve neither us nor our children.

Parents with nurturing teaching styles realize that their children always require their attention and care. They are flexible in responding toward their children to accommodate their child's individual differences and developmental progression. Children are far more likely to keep in touch with and express their essential natures when guided in this way. Such children build and retain confidence, creativity and self-acceptance, all potent contributors to self-empowerment.

CHAPTER 6

Tools of the Parent/Teacher

In addition to being clear about their parental roles, the significant qualities parents need are *patience,[1] acceptance,[2] openness* **and** *truthfulness.* Employing these qualities is a magnificent way to plant and nurture all of your child's seeds! Parents then subtly and profoundly teach these attributes to their children.

Children are like tape recorders. Physiologically, their brain waves are much slower but with higher amplitudes than those of most adults. Unless adults are deep meditators, their brain waves are much more frequent with lower amplitudes than those of children. Adult minds are busy with thoughts centered in the past or future. Children center in the present and constantly gather in all types of information. Not only are they listening to what you are saying, but are also absorbing how you are saying it, how you are feeling

---

[1]　Patience is the ability to understand and to work harmoniously with natural law and natural cycles.

[2]　Acceptance is unconditionally believing that," Whatever is happening or presenting in the moment is most appropriate." It is equally important to consider that whatever we are feeling or being in the moment is largely a result of our conditioning and is also appropriate. When we accept unconditionally and do not judge our feelings, our realities or our thoughts (and those of others) as good/bad or right/wrong, we allow ourselves to assume the wise and empowering position of the observer. As observer, the opportunity is present to make discerning observations concerning the truthfulness of our assumptions and our beliefs. Equally empowering is the fact that we then give ourselves a choice as to how we respond to what is happening in that moment, rather than unconsciously reacting out of habit.

when you say it, and what is happening at the time you say it. With this *subtle*[3] information, they formulate their *concepts*[4] of physical reality that they draw upon in order to function within this world. Children can be *intuitive*[5] at a young age—that is, unless self-doubt and illusion are sowed or implanted into their belief systems. Therefore, when you, as a parent, express yourself in genuine patience, acceptance and truthfulness, you are collaborating with your children's natural intuitiveness.

When any relationship—be it between parent and child, teacher and student, lovers, or friends—is built upon authenticity, it becomes a positive and powerful alliance. Though rarely able to express it, most children sense when adults are genuine and when they are not. When children sense that relationships with their parents are honest and secure, they are far more able to trust the guidance of their parents and to feel safe to be their *Authentic Selves.*[6]

Openness, patience, acceptance and truthfulness cannot be overestimated between parent and child. They are crucial principles for parents to consider, understand and integrate into their family structure for their children's successful psycho-social and psycho-spiritual development. The next four chapters will be devoted to these key qualities of successful parenting.

---

[3]   Subtle refers to what is not easily perceived with the physical senses of touch, taste, sight, hearing, and smell.

[4]   A concept is a general understanding of something.

[5]   Intuitive refers to one who is sensitive and can interpret energetic communications.

[6]   Our Authentic Self is the self that seeks joyful and genuine expression through living physical life. It has been defined by some as the "Soul," and by others as the "Higher Self" or "God Self." It is the energy of the Authentic Self that animates and brings life to the physical body. (See glossary for further information.)

CHAPTER 7

Openness

Openness is the quality that calls forth change and growth and invites the blossoming of the Authentic Self. **When you are open, you are saying to the Universe, "I invite whatever situations or people into my life that will lead ultimately to my psycho-spiritual development."** When this honest proclamation reaches the subtle ears of the Universe, you bring to yourself the blessings and challenges that will fulfill your deepest desires to live life fully.

Openness, when owned by parents and accepted as a quality benefiting their children, plants a seed that encourages their sons and daughters to meet life as it unfolds, accepting and using situations that arise as opportunities to learn and improve their life skills.

Because it is innate in children to a great extent, openness is a quality that does not need to be taught, but rather is one that should be gently nurtured and guarded. Children generally demonstrate openness by their strong desire to learn and experience new things. Being open and dealing with the world in its current chaotic state can be difficult, however. How do we as parents help our sons and daughters with this seemingly daunting task? As aware parents, we want our sons and daughters to be open to their own creative and explorative processes and the gifts of life, without being exploited. Part of the answer lies in further understanding the development of healthy boundaries in our children. In Chapter 5, *Parenting Styles,* we touched upon parents establishing age-appropriate parameters to provide their children with safe surroundings to learn about their environment and society and to practice interacting with it. These boundaries are central to nurturing and guarding their openness.

A good metaphor for openness with beneficial boundaries is the natural and healthy workings of a cell membrane. The membrane permits the required elements necessary for physical health and stability to permeate into the cell's inner chamber. A healthy cell membrane also keeps out the harmful substances to the physical mechanics that sustain the delicate balance of health and life. When a virus, such as the common cold attacks our system, it tricks the cell membranes into thinking the virus is harmless. The viral invader penetrates into the cell and our physical body and our natural healthy physical state experiences temporary havoc. Even though a healthy cell membrane is occasionally fooled, the immune system learns the virus's chemical composition and nature so that it will not enter the cell again.

The mental/emotional parts of us have corresponding capabilities that are similar to the workings of a physically healthy human cell. In this analogy, the psychological and spiritual acumen we gain from struggling with and learning from situations that affect our mental/emotional health is much like the physical body's immune system when it encounters a virus. If the immune system of our subtle body develops appropriately, we will allow growth-producing situations into our reality while keeping out or managing disadvantageous ones. The "white blood cells" of our subtle immune system are pieces of wisdom and knowledge, which help us differentiate between what is useful and what is not for our greater benefit.

Wisdom allows us to develop strong and intelligent boundaries, but at the same time these boundaries are flexible and fluid. For instance, a 12-year-old daughter has known and been friendly with another 12 year-old girl for most of her life. The other girl, however, is now connected with a group who experiments with drugs. How does your daughter handle this situation? Does she turn her back on her friend and condemn her, setting up an isolating "good" and "bad" separating situation? It is my feeling that abandoning a friend in this way because her choices are not ones you would make serves no one. Often drug use is self-medication for a far deeper conflict. In this case, a flexible and fluid boundary for your daughter might be that she continues to be kind and *compassionate*[1] toward her friend, but understands the consequences of this activity for herself. Although she is still open to the other girl, she is aware that for her to be pulled into a situation with drugs is not helpful. In this way, your daughter is discerning, but is not afraid to allow something new or challenging to penetrate her life.

Parents often teach their mental/emotional boundaries to their children by example. These parental seeds are planted, often unconsciously, simply

---

[1] Compassion is having deep respect and honor for another's journey.

because their children's tape recorder minds are on. When parents are alert to the state of their own boundaries, and are committed to developing in their own wisdom, they teach their children by example how to recognize and work with fears that often limit openness.

For instance, it is possible for an unaware mother's fear of water, resulting from a traumatic, near-drowning incident that happened in her own childhood, to be unconsciously transferred to her child. The mother may react with apparent anxiety when a situation triggers her fears. The woman's boundaries may be such that she does not allow herself to enter situations that activate her dread of water. She may not travel on or over an ocean; she may not go swimming or even go wading; she may not ride in a boat on a quiet lake or even sit by a river. Her boundaries are hyper-vigilant in keeping her safe, which in this case could be considered *neurotic*.[2] If the mother is equally overly frightened with respect to her child's connection with water and is not aware of the power her own associations have on him/her, the child may assume his/her mother's fear of water and her resistant and impermeable boundary. The mother involuntarily passes on a belief that limits her child's mastery of the world.

A less obvious example of a parental boundary that might be transferred to a child is that of a responsible and hard-working father who is fearful of making a change in his miserable employment situation. This hypothetical father fears that if he speaks up at his work or quits, nothing else will be there for him. Because he has low self-confidence, this father consequently stays in unhappy circumstances. This man is representing porous boundaries. Because of his fear of not being worthy and his assumption of disaster, he allows others to take advantage of him. The man's child may not have learned insecurity and self-doubt through his/her own personal experience but is witnessing the father's unhealthy boundaries and how he copes.

In the above two instances, the parents were not aware of the state of their boundaries. When the parents are aware of them, their impact on their children are lessened. They are then able to give their children, especially when they are older, a healthier perspective of a situation. The information

---

[2]   Neurosis is no longer recognized as a scientific term; however we use the word in this book to describe the formation of behavioral or psychosomatic symptoms as a result of repressed data and emotions being contacted. A person becomes neurotic when his ego has lost the capacity to keep buried information and emotions tucked away in the unconscious or subconscious. Symptoms of neurosis are depression, fear, anger, jealousy, grief, hate, etc.

the child is witnessing does not go into his/her data banks without qualifying information.

There are also tangible ways to exemplify and foster openness. One way is to **remind your child often, "If you want to know anything from me, just ask." Then be open to any question, no matter what it might be.** This shows your child that there are no inappropriate questions. It does not mean that you will know all of the answers, but if not, tell your child you will find out. This keeps your child's curiosity and thirst for exploration and knowledge open and healthy.

It is important in this paradigm to know that neither parents nor children must be perfect. This paradigm's basic premise is that we are all learning and evolving, including grownups. The gift that parents can truthfully impart to their children is to admit their challenges and model ways to meet them courageously. This requires a certain amount of *vulnerability*[3] to say to ourselves and to our children, "I am working on this myself and I don't have all of the answers, but I do know it is okay to admit this and to take it slow."

Another exercise adults can practice with their child to foster healthy openness is to ask him/her daily, "Tell me about yourself." This open-ended opportunity does not limit what he/she can talk about in response. When asked regularly by a parent, a youngster receives the message that he/she is included and important in the parent's life. This strengthens the foundation of a child's self-concept and directly adds to his/her level of healthy openness.

With this exercise, children are allowed the space to contact their inner selves and attempt to verbally explain their perceptions about themselves. When children focus on themselves for even a brief time, they develop skills of self-observation, which, in turn, promotes self-knowledge. Self-knowledge leads to a stronger sense of self and is an important foundational ingredient of openness.

It may be difficult for parents to hear what their children might express. Because of their innocence and immaturity, they may not say what is on their minds in what parents might consider a socially accepted manner. It is important that parents accept whatever their children say without hasty criticism. That is not to say that parents cannot discuss the merits of their children's thoughts, but children often take criticism as an assault on them personally.

---

[3] Vulnerability is the state of being totally open and forthright. This state of being is extremely threatening to our personalities and our egos, but when subtle energetics is understood, there is an absolute knowledge that great power is inherent in any moment we represent ourselves authentically.

It will be much easier to allow children to tell you what they are contemplating without judgment if you first understand a little bit about the mind and how it works. If you were to stop your own mind for a moment and truthfully tell someone what you were thinking, your thoughts may sound quite absurd. The mind communicates in symbols that rarely make sense to rational intelligence. We generally process these symbols, clean them up for the public, and put them into our socially accepted, but very limited, language.

Children have yet to develop the means to censor or control expression of their thoughts and ideas. However, those who are given the opportunity to talk about their feelings and thoughts to their parents become those rare individuals who are in touch with, and can creatively and succinctly, express their inner selves.

It is important that parents keep in mind that they and their children are at different levels of openness. Because adults have sometimes become hardened as a result of childhood and life experiences, they may be involuntarily fearful, wary and overly cautious. However, by utilizing simple techniques described in this chapter and being aware of their own openness and boundaries, parents then place emphasis on their children's wholesome growth and expansion.

CHAPTER 8

Patience

Many adults have the tendency to hurry things, but **rushing a child ahead of his/her normal cadence in mental, emotional or physical development can create a psychological scar.**

If a child is slow to develop his physical skills, such as riding a bicycle or playing a sport, it will do no good to expect him/her to be as proficient as those to whom it comes easy. The byproduct of hurrying a child or commanding him/her beyond his/her capabilities is frustration, self-doubt and competitiveness. He/she may try very hard to meet your demands and develop ways to appease you, but expecting the unobtainable from a child always creates scars.

Forcing (as opposed to encouraging) a child can result in anxiety disorders in adulthood. Pushed children either may shy away from any kind of group activity for fear of failing or may be fiercely competitive. They rely on success to define their self-worth.

All of us have witnessed parents of cheerleaders, or of soccer, football, basketball, or other sport players who demand that their children be on the team, get all of the playing time, and receive awards. Under what kind of pressure are their children? How much energy is left for their sons and daughters to discover and develop into who they are? Forcing a little girl to play soccer might preclude her growing into being a master artist, because the development of intuition and inspiration for her artistry was side-lined.

Pushing their children is a difficult habit for parents to break. For some it is an addiction. It is tied directly to acceptance, which will be addressed in more depth in Chapter 9. Many parents who anxiously push their child are convinced that if their son or daughter does not excel, their child's future is doomed.

Parents often react subconsciously to the pressure they felt as children. Many feel that they let down their parents. This perceived failure as children by parents often surfaces undetected in some father-son, mother-daughter situations.

The father of a high school football player once told his child's coach that he did not know what overcame him when his son played poorly. He admitted that his rage was so consuming that he would belittle his son, pushing the boy to get angry enough to "play like a man." The son was bewildered by his father's anger and admitted he had considered suicide. He felt doomed in his efforts to be good enough to please his father. Imagine the disfigurement to the young man's psyche, and what the father must have experienced in his childhood to act this way toward his son.

Some boys gravitate naturally to football and playing it comes easily to them. If they enjoy participating in the sport, this indicates a good match for them.

As in all areas of parenting, patience is a matter of listening to get to know your children: Their potentials; their inherent challenges; and their likes and dislikes. Listening cultivates awareness of what is really happening within them. As a parent, it is equally important to understand your unconscious motivations. The football father is a regrettable and clear example of a parent recreating his childhood wound in his own son. Though the actions of many other parents are not as apparent as those of this particular father, their effects can be just as disastrous.

Patient parents will focus on their children's inner development rather than achievements gained through competition. Inner development depends largely on learning to face obstacles and life challenges with composure. Therefore, **instructing our children that whatever happens in life can be handled teaches them patience toward and acceptance of themselves and their world. When parents teach and personally hold this conviction, their children learn by example to take command of their lives without fear of failure.**

In our own experiences of unexpected happenings, we often look back and see that we needed a change, and our lives were enriched by facing what seemed to be a disappointment or setback. Therefore, depending on your child's maturity level, share a personal story when this proved true in your life. Children love stories! Parents can teach the wisdom of the saying: "When God (Universe) closes a door, He (It) always opens a window."

If your son or daughter is having difficulty with a developmental issue, social situation or a subject in school, say to your child, "You've hit a snag, and I'll help you work through it." Patience and acceptance allow the child to begin developing appropriate standards and tools to overcome obstacles. This is the mark of a skilled teaching parent.

When gently guided, children brought up in the environment of patience and acceptance quickly learn also to work in effective groups and teams, utilizing the skills and potentials of everyone in the group. **In developing a generation that understands the principle of cooperation and harmony, we raise the consciousness of humankind.** Children who have been guided in this way automatically attract others of like mind. Even though their numbers may be small initially, their groups will have a profound rippling impact on the world.

CHAPTER 9

Acceptance

Acceptance is closest to what I define as *unconditional love*[1] in this book.

Unconditional love embraces the entire expression of another individual, whether or not that individual conforms to your beliefs of what is appropriate or what is supposed to be.

Parents are challenged to create a haven at home that supports unconditional acceptance of their children's identities and the unfoldment of their destinies. How? Merely by knowing that their children are unique and have individual destinies with distinct challenges to meet and master. Parents can then listen with discerning ears and become creative in helping their children meet their physical, social, psychological and spiritual needs.

In the family, the pinnacle of acceptance and self-acceptance is knowing that "What is, is"—and there is really no good or bad judgment to be made. We may not understand why our children have particular characteristics or talents, or why they are meeting the challenges that come their way. If we trust, however, that whatever is unfolding is the expression of their evolutionary path, we tend to be more patient, more accepting, more helpful . . . and much less judgmental. It is then easier to assist our child in understanding consequences and making wise choices.

Parents steeped in the old beliefs that children should be "perfect" initially are likely to experience anxiety if their children do fit what they consider is the accepted norm. The parents' inner programming will scream that this

---

[1] Unconditional love, as closely as we can understand it, is total acceptance of whatever has emerged without judgment or urge to necessarily fix it or dispose of it.

will be the cause of their child's downfall. What if their son or daughter will not fit into society and its system of acceptance, achievement and rewards? **Society's institutions and systems must and will change and evolve with the emergence of children's creative, inclusive natures.**

Pioneers who influenced humanity with their innovative and creative thought and ideas frequently did not "fit in" as children. Several schools refused Dr. Einstein admission because he did not fit their criteria. Because of his non-traditional ideas and strong sense of self and purpose, he challenged many teachers and systems. However, he never lost himself, even when things appeared hopeless. He and other true heroes had the inner strength to withstand the societal pressures to conform and become forces of expansion.

Nothing is more destructive to the tender psyches of children than *judgment.*[2] Judgment is so potent that one (especially a parent) does not have to say anything for their children to sense and record internally their parents' criticism. Parental judgments often leave scars, creating underlying self-doubts that can inhibit their youngsters throughout life.

From where does judgment originate? Perhaps from life philosophies and religions which teach that one must conform to particular doctrines and strict behavioral constraints. Such inflexible and judgmental philosophies and religions can create division because actions or beliefs are viewed as right or wrong, good or bad. Children instead will benefit from being guided in more flexible terms, such as what is most helpful to them and what is not.

Many adults have a difficult time if their children do not adhere to a set of behavioral standards. Parents often feel judged as good or bad parents solely by how well their children behave, or how "nice" they act in the presence of others.

One mother worried that her 7-year-old daughter did not understand compassion. The mother's concern arose when her child verbally observed that a handicapped child was physically different from other children. Although her daughter was simply trying to make sense of her world, the parent was distraught because she thought that her daughter was insensitive. The mother had been taught that it is rude to comment on differences in others.

The mother condemned the actions of the child for not acting compassionate and this confused the child. Being compassionate and

---

[2]   Judgment is a tool of discerning thought that when used in a negative way, automatically sets up moralistic thought and separative dynamics. This happens when one thinks in terms of good or bad, right or wrong, righteous or sinner, better than or worse than. Genuine acceptance and compassion cannot coexist in a mind that is judgmental.

"acting" nice are not synonymous. It would have been better if the mother had understood the child's intent instead of assuming that she meant to hurt another. Parents can take such opportunities by asking further questions to ascertain if the child intended malice.

Assisting the child in clarifying her intentions and thoughts can be of great help, and it opens a door for discussion of other potential ways to handle these situations. It is also an excellent opportunity to talk about the blessing of differences in individuals. Children easily learn it is okay to openly discuss differences in others and themselves, understanding that everyone is unique and has a contribution to make.

As we develop this sense of acceptance, we, as parents, do several things: We teach our children compassion for and acceptance of others—and most importantly, we make it possible for them to also have compassion toward themselves. We thus provide a nurturing and encouraging environment.

Many adults were raised with *conditional love*[3] because their parents believed children must be molded for their own good into "the perfect child." It was common to believe that the most expedient way to do this was by withholding and bartering with what they craved most—parental love and acceptance.

An important contribution to their children's healthy psycho-spiritual and psycho-social development by today's parents is true acceptance of their intrinsic dispositions. In contrast to conditional love, **unconditional love fosters a deep, rich trust between parent and child.** Parents become nurturers, assisting their children develop as confident, well-adjusted and happy individuals. Although unable to verbally express it, children sense when adults are sincerely patient, accepting and truthful. Without fanfare, children then quietly blossom, because this natural process is encouraged and supported.

---

[3]   Conditional love—or conditional acceptance—is more a conditioning tool than an emotion. It is based on the concept that, "I will love you if you please me." Conditional love is the prime reason we have lost our direction in matters of the heart. The word "love" automatically triggers the soft states of acceptance, but conditional love has little to do with the heart. It is manipulative and is a mind game.

CHAPTER 10

Truthfulness

We have talked about the intuitiveness of children. Consider their sharp insight when you are reluctant to share with them your true thoughts and *emotions*,[1] and the truth about situations that in some way affect them.

Children learn to communicate primarily from their parents or other adults. They may learn healthy communication skills of negotiation, discussion, and openness in sharing emotions. On the other hand, when intuitive and sensitive children receive imprecise and complicated messages from adults, their natural sense of order is thrown off balance.

Parents and other adults may try to keep the truth from children because they do not know how to be honest without causing confusion or hurt. Many adults also want to shield children from the harsh side of reality. **It is important for adults to remember that children can deal with just about anything if told in an objective and compassionate way.** Of course, a small child will have to be told simply in terms he or she can understand. An older child will be capable of more in-depth understanding, but also will require additional assistance in dealing with his or her more complex assumptions and associated emotions.

For example, a conscientious father of a 16-old son and 6-year-old daughter is unexpectedly laid off from his job. For most men, facing this situation is difficult because they may feel they are not in control of their

---

[1]   Emotions are complex and sometimes strong subjective responses. When feeling a strong emotional reaction, physiologic changes actually occur that prepares the individual who is feeling the strong emotion for physical action. Strong emotions result when something happens or someone does something that is unexpected.

lives or are not valued in their work. The father in the example may also fear losing face in his family. How he handles the situation can either help pull the family together or fuel a stressful situation.

The father understands that his children's lives will be affected by the layoff. Their daily routines will most likely change, and the stress of such a major change almost certainly will cause emotional ups and downs for both parents and children. In addition to the change in their daily routines, perhaps an anticipated family activity such as a Disneyland vacation may have to be cancelled.

The father may choose to first confide in his wife to release any emotions of fear, anger, guilt, or hurt. To first express and become aware of and put his emotions into perspective is important, because the father can then speak with his children more objectively and answer their questions with composure.

After working through his initial emotions, the father may talk to his 6-year-old daughter saying, "I've been laid off from my work, so I will be looking for another job." He can tell her about any specific changes that may affect her. Then the father can address and answer any concerns or questions his daughter has as honestly and simply as possible.

At age 6, children do not generally fear or get angry as adults do. In the above example, the father's initial communication to his daughter is truthful and forthright, and in the language 6-year-olds can understand. The father has conveyed openness by asking his daughter if she has any questions, and he communicates his future availability to her. All of his daughter's later concerns or inquiries equally can be dealt with honestly, sincerely and directly.

In talking to his 16-year-old son, the father may have to explain in more detail about the situation and about emotional issues. As children mature, they develop beliefs, ego defenses and a portfolio of emotional reactions that are stored subconsciously. The sudden unemployment of his father can be extremely disturbing to a 16-year-old, triggering subconscious fears and anxieties the teenager may not be able to understand or express. The father needs to explain in more detail how the situation of being laid off occurred. He may also have to explain how he is handling it practically and emotionally. By being honest and composed in telling his 16-year-old about the situation, he is modeling a way to work constructively through an upsetting life circumstance.

A boy's father is his most important role model in facing the world outside his family. Even though adolescent behavior often clouds the child's acknowledgment of such lessons, if he later faces similar situations, he will naturally draw on his father's example.

In being honest and explaining to their children within the scope of their ability to understand, parents are best guided by the questions posed by their children. When they have addressed their children's concerns, parents can then gently have them review what they understood from the exchange in order to clarify any lingering misunderstandings. If this crucial step is missing, any misinterpretations children take away from the interchange begin to take on a life of their own within their minds.

Consider the same hypothetical family in yet another situation. In this scenario, the mother and father are experiencing marital problems. The parents' conflict has escalated to a point where their children's interests are secondary to the marital friction, and the tension now affects the children's home life. The perceptive parents agree that it is important to talk with their children to clarify the situation for them, without which the conflict might become frightful and worrisome in children's minds.

There is nothing more important to children than their parents and the relationship between their parents. The truth of any matter is seldom as ominous as what the child's mind has made it out to be. With few exceptions, feuding moms and dads rarely realize the intense ramifications their relationship difficulties have on their children's sense of security and wellbeing. Without careful explanation to the contrary, children will add to their stress by blaming themselves for trouble within their parents' marriage.

Parents can sensitively explain the crux of their serious marital friction to their children without blaming his/her partner. They should strongly point out that their adult problems are not the responsibility of their children. Perhaps the adults have a deep ongoing difference of opinion or are growing apart. Perhaps something has happened that makes living together difficult and perhaps unlikely. Even if parents are considering divorce, it is important to be as honest as possible with their children. Even though a divorce can be devastating initially for children, being untruthful about it can make it a terrible experience for them.

When the relationship of the parents is troubled, but they are both committed to being protectors of their children's best interests, children adapt more easily to any changes that happen within the family structure. It is routinely said that children would rather be "from" a broken home rather than be "in" one. It is crucial that children, of any age, know *they* are not being divorced and both parents are committed to their welfare.

Children need an opportunity to have their questions and concerns answered, and their misconceptions clarified. When parents lovingly and objectively communicate their issues and life challenges with their children, they model one of the most essential life skills—how to manage otherwise devastating situations.

Language and self-expression are integral to effectively employing truthfulness as a parental tool and teaching it as a laudable quality to children. These topics will be the focus of the next chapter.

CHAPTER 11

The Power of Language

Everything pulsates with an energetic vibration—objects, people, thoughts, emotions, actions and especially words. In this chapter, the *energetic dynamics*[1] and *mind patterns*[2] that surround the intertwining of emotions and actions with words will be explored.

Recall a time when something that someone said to you made your inner intuition stand at alert. Perhaps you sensed that what the individual thought was not what he/she said, or possibly the person said one thing but his/her actions said another. What you probably experienced was a dissonance of vibrations.

When this happens, we are confused, leaving an impression of disharmony or distrust. **Our inner sense of vibrational equilibrium and balance attempts to harmonize the discord.** Without being aware of it, we try to make sense of the situation. Most of the time, adults are unconscious of this inner harmonizing process. We usually form a rationale to explain the disharmony, which may or may not be accurate.

In our need to make sense of and dismiss an uncomfortable experience, we make assumptions. Mystery novels exemplify this. In a mystery, one explanation usually stands out. Although there may be strong support for the most rational explanation, what seems most plausible may not be what actually happened. The reader must sometimes follow obscure clues to solve the mystery.

---

[1] Energy movement and flow and its resulting effects and transformations.

[2] Mind patterns are patterns of beliefs and thoughts that create our reactions and our life experiences. For instance, if we are naturally happy and believe we will be fortunate in life, that mind pattern will manifest itself. On the other hand, if we believe we are always being slighted, that mind pattern will also manifest itself.

To absorb as much information as possible, our minds devise shortcuts and make assumptions. For example, we are constantly bombarded by advertising, which often plays on our fears, securities and desires. Advertisers hope we believe we need what they have to offer to be safe, liked, happy, healthy or rich.

Auto ads frequently show a macho man driving a car with a breathtakingly beautiful woman looking adoringly at him. Why? The advertisers are seeding the subconscious with the association that the car is what will make a man sexy. This association raises the potential that men in the advertiser's target group will buy the car that is being advertised instead of employing more practical considerations in their choices.

A consequence of our inattentiveness toward what is being communicated to us has been that meanings of words have been corrupted, especially those words surrounding *feelings.*[3]

Footnotes and a *glossary*[4] at the back of this book define key words with the meanings that I have attached to them. Define for yourself these key words before reading the footnote or consulting the glossary. This exercise will show how differently people understand and use routine words.

When children are small, whatever words are associated with the general emotional and physical vibrations they receive contribute to their own inner glossary of terms and meanings. We are often unaware of the associations that children make as we communicate with them. It might astonish us to know the concepts and mind patterns children have construed and tucked into their own inner glossary.

Programs such as *Kids Say The Darnedest Things,* Art Linkletter's and Bill Cosby's TV partnership with young children, have shown us how youngsters interpret their observations and what they have heard from adults. Teachers are also often a rich source of similar stories. For example, a student wrote in a school essay, "The human body is composed of three parts: the Brainium, the Borax, and the Abdominable Cavity. The Branium contains the brain. The Borax contains the lungs, the liver, and the living things. The Abdominable Cavity contains the bowels, of which there are five: A,E,I,O, and U."

---

[3]   Feelings are emotional responses that cause a reaction. This reaction can be positive, opening the heart to vibrate with joy and happiness. The reaction can also be negative causing our hearts to close down and protect itself. This prompts us to be defensive, attacking or controlling.

[4]   A list of words and an explanation of their meanings that allow a deeper understanding of subtle concepts presented in a body of text.

Another anecdote: One day a student announced to his class, "My aunt won't be having any more kids because her tubes are tired!" This instance shows how a child will combine bits and pieces of his knowledge and add it to his inner glossary.

It is cute and entertaining to hear some of the remarkable associations that children have begun to store in their minds as facts. Many of these associations will be clarified as a child gains maturity and proceeds in his educational process. However, **many definitions and concepts associated with feelings become powerful seeds implanted in their minds, and will become profoundly influential in the overall life blueprint of their lives.**

It is important that parents help children understand language and especially help them find words to express feelings and emotions. For many children, if they cry or act out to express themselves, they often will be told that those reactions are not appropriate. Children are left with only one option, which is to bury their emotions and their not-understood bewildering causes in their subconscious. Here they fester. Repressed emotions drain valuable energy—energy that could be used more appropriately to discover and create.

Love[5] is a powerfully emotional word. What we associate with the word love in our early years forms our deepest concept of it. The conflict between what we experience as children and what we innately know love to be often must be addressed as adults in psychotherapy. When the issues and experiences that surround this conflict can be isolated and successfully processed, changes take place in a person's psycho-spiritual makeup, greatly influencing his relationship with himself and with others.

Consider a little boy whose mother is self-absorbed and whose parenting style is neglectful. The mother says, "I love you," to the child, but her behavior is distant and cold. The child's earliest experience of love thus has associations of emotional distance. Neglect and emotional distance do not resonate with love. As the boy grows, he will likely face conflict about love in many of his relationships.

---

[5]   Love has many meanings, and while most are highly charged emotionally, many of them carry a lot of negative baggage, e.g., emotional addictions. Addictions are more accurately defined in terms of "attachment" rather than "love." However, when one is experiencing a high vibration of love, there is nothing like it. In that moment, the person feels at one with everything, the energetic connection is profound, and negativity is nonexistent. Because we are in a physical dimension, we often experience gradients of this high vibrational emotion and our hearts open to share without expecting reciprocity.

These muddled associations usually lie in the unconscious or subconscious, and rarely do we realize their impact on our lives. In the example above, this child-as-adult will probably find himself in relationships that reflect and reinforce feelings of low self-worth and self-love. He may subconsciously try to work through these issues by entering into relationships with partners who are distant and neglectful. Or, he may attract a smothering partner as an attempt to compensate the lack of affection he felt.

How can we be positive influences and teach healthy communication to our children? First, as addressed earlier in this book, we can **be honest in thought, word and deed with ourselves and our children.** Even if we are not always model parents, if we are truthful, we help our children develop the tools to be honest with themselves. Children will then have a helpful technique in their own coping repertoire that prepares them to deal with life challenges.

It is a phenomenal gift to teach a child that, although this world is not perfect, he/she has the power to accept, take responsibility for, and change his/her personal, subjective life situations.

Second, **it is important that as their children mature and become more verbally proficient, that parents check their children's understanding around specific meanings of words and associated concepts.** Parents often assume that their sons and daughters perceive things in the same way that they, as adults, perceive them. This often is not the case.

In asking our children non-judgmental questions about what they think about and how they comprehend their world, we open the door to increasing their clarity of understanding. It additionally helps them build a vocabulary to express their emotions and thoughts. Parents can offer more concise definitions of words or concepts that become a part of the child's inner glossary. Parents also will have an opportunity to clarify misconceptions their children may have around themselves and their environment.

My father used to say, **"You can't put a man's head on a child's shoulders."** This wisdom greatly influenced my thinking regarding children. In many instances, we assume children can reason and conceptualize in complex ways, when actually they are actively absorbing bits and pieces of information and their intellectual and analytical faculties are just developing. We would not expect a kindergartner to be able to understand a doctoral class. Even though a child can be taught to mimic words, his understanding of concepts and meanings of complex ideas has not yet developed. **Maturation processes are very individualistic.**

Third, **talk with your child. Listen to your child.** We greatly rely on words to communicate. Listen also to what your child is saying non-verbally in body language or actions. These nonverbal indicators are often the accurate communications of how he/she genuinely feels and how he/she perceives his/her world.

For instance, your normally gregarious daughter tells you nothing is bothering her but spends most of the weekend her room. Two things happen when you, the caring parent, talk to your daughter about your observations. She observes herself and what she is doing; and she has an opportunity to explain what she is feeling and what is going on for her. When her words are not consistent with her actions, help your daughter bring her words into congruency with her feelings. Note that I said, *bring her words into congruency with her feelings*, and not vice versa. If you ask your daughter what is going on with her and she answers, "I'll be okay. Don't worry about me," you can help her explain what she is actually feeling and the reasons behind her feelings. As parents, you do not have to fix anything for your youngster. Helping your child express her feelings helps her with the first step in working through her situation.

Fourth, **be aware of what you say about yourself, your partner and others when you are around your children.** Some of us are self-deprecating and/or hostile or disrespectful toward others. We plant "seeds," and our children record these judgments as facts in their inner glossary.

If we are intent upon clear communications with our children, it is wise to state information as clearly as possible. This does not mean that we cannot or should not express our feelings and own them, but it does mean that we be mindful of making public our judgments of ourselves or others based solely on habit or upon emotional reaction. We should state information, our perceptions and our feelings without emotional *drama*[6] attached.

Language and words are powerful tools that can plant either positive or negative seeds. A word or phrase can start panic in a crowd or incite a mob. Conversely, a word or phrase can calm a crowd and soothe a heart.

---

[6] Drama refers to the soap opera reality we usually find ourselves in when we participate in negative emotional games. These games involve the negative type of emotions such as judgment, greed, lust, fear, hate, jealousy, control, revenge, competition, etc. (See glossary for further explanation.)

When we teach children words, we invite all sorts of associations to enter their minds. They receive the totality of what we are transmitting, consciously or unconsciously, via a *communication package.*[7] Associations made by children often are unchallenged. As parents become more aware of this, they help keep the fertile soil of their children's minds less cluttered by clearly explaining the meaning of words. This is an important step in their cognitive development.

Parents can use language in conscious ways to initiate and reinforce helpful subconscious patterning. In the next chapter, we will explore ways to do this as we discuss the use of family decrees.

---

[7]   A communication package is a collective of the ways we communicate our thoughts, our emotions, and our state of energetic balance outwardly, both subtly and in more commonly recognizable ways. People rely heavily upon the spoken word in their communication. Words are extremely powerful and can be quite helpful. However, they can also become a tool to deceive or control others. Those who are intuitive (and many children are before they are taught to discredit this profound tool) are also picking up and reacting to the state of the energetic field. When we are able to interpret the energy field correctly, we tap into the clearest form of communication.

CHAPTER 12

Family Decrees

Family decrees are uncomplicated family philosophies to which the whole family commits. The practiced principles become valuable tools that, when repeated often, become useful habits of thinking. Family decrees give children dependable inner guidance that positively influences their lives. Children may forget the decrees when initially introduced. They may not remember them for the first year, or even for the first five years. If consistently taught, however, a strong foundation forms in their consciousnesses, an underpinning that will be owned throughout their entire lifetimes.

An example of a familiar principle is the Boy Scouts motto *Be Prepared*. This Scouts' principle is a powerful philosophy that permeates the organization, and the motto has successfully influenced the lives of many of its members. **Often what we learn as children, by both word and by deed, form our habits, thoughts and beliefs throughout our entire lives.**

A positive decree a family might adopt is, **"Be calm first, then speak."** This philosophy can be one of the most empowering seeds to which we expose our children. Teaching them to be able to stop and arrive at calmness teaches stillness and listening, and creates the pause necessary to decide on an appropriate response or reply. A related family decree could be, **"When you feel yourself losing control or reacting, take a deep breath."**

In life, if we can pause for an instant without reacting to a situation or to another person, the hesitation provides a moment to make a mindful, centered decision or response. The family decree establishes the habit of conscious speaking rather than unconscious reaction. How many times have we wished to take back what we said? A deep breath will tend to restore *composure,*[1] which allows us to be in control of the moment rather than being controlled by our reactions or the actions of others.

"Be helpful," is a good family philosophy that teaches compassion and teamwork. This principle also generates what might be considered *good karma.*[2] However, it is appropriate to caution children that some people will reject an offer of help. This provides an opportunity to discuss with children the rights of others to choose whether they want help and to honor that choice. Sometimes, allowing another to be independent is the best way to respect and honor that individual.

Still another family practice might be, **"We will be available to help each other in making wise choices."** This teaches wisdom, trust and teamwork. Yet another decree might be, **"Everyone has a right to his/her opinions."** This instills tolerance and acceptance. An especially good philosophy for all in the family is, **"Everyone has a right to a time-out to think things through."** This allows for control, intermission, patience and self-observation.

A family decree consciously frames the family together to a strong, understood, positive, single focus. It is important that parents commit to these decrees. As we discussed earlier, children are like tape recorders; they absorb all of your words, feelings and actions. If parents exemplify, respond and *commit*[3] to these philosophies, children are more likely to do so. Another family decree might be, **"When we make a commitment, we do everything in our power to keep it."** Commitment is a large part of the foundation of success. If we are not committed to our work, our family, our community

---

[1] Composure denotes self-awareness, self-possession and calmness even in the face of distractions and excitable situations.

[2] Good karma results when both the giver and the receiver benefit from the act of good will. Simply put, good karma is the positive dynamic that exemplifies the old saying, "You reap what you sow." It illustrates the principle of cause and effect.

[3] Commitment refers to a pledge to keep an agreement or accomplish a course of action successfully. A commitment is an agreement that you make to yourself, but does not necessarily benefit others. It is important to understand what one can be responsible for in terms of making a commitment. For instance, if one promises to make the other happy, this is not a realistic commitment. One does not (and cannot) possess the power to make another happy. One can create a diversion in another's life that for a time will supersede or overshadow unhappiness, but one's own happiness is one's own responsibility.

or to taking care of ourselves, we are diverted from our intended course. As children begin to understand the word and meaning of commitment, parents must strive to *impeccably*[4] model its congruency, both in word and in deed. Thus, the dedication of parents to the family decrees provides an excellent model of commitment for their children.

Family decrees are positive and valuable philosophical "seeds." Although decrees are most effective when started at an early age, it is never too late to begin. At any age, defining and committing to family decrees positively influences family relationships and dynamics. **These family philosophies form pillars that each member, when feeling threatened or lost, will remember to regain perspective and balance.**

---

[4] Impeccable means flawless. Here it means using precise and exact words, which truthfully and clearly express both thoughts and feelings.

CHAPTER 13

Managing Emotions

Emotions set the tone of virtually all life experiences. These potent forces, in large part, determine our actions, influence even our important life decisions, and give meaning to our lives. Emotions can be our guides to assist in what gives us pleasure and what makes us feel fulfilled. *Joseph Campbell*[1] pointed out often in his many lectures and books that in order for our lives to be complete or fulfilled, we must follow our bliss. I understand "bliss" to mean the spiritual joy felt when we connect to our greater selves and our greater mission. We can learn about the power of emotions and use positive emotions to assist in our journey of "following our bliss" to meet with our greatest destiny.

Emotions also are the forces that imprint our lasting impressions of shocking experiences. If emotions caused by these experiences go unmanaged, they often take up residence in our subconscious and rob us of our individuality.

For instance, if a purse-snatcher steals a woman's purse during her usually safe walk home from work, her belief that the world is safe probably changes

---

[1] Joseph Campbell (1904-1987) was an author and lifelong student and professor of the human spirit and comparative mythology. At the time of his death, Newsweek Magazine noted that, "Campbell has become one of the rarest of intellectuals in American Life: A serious thinker who has been embraced by the popular culture." Two excellent books by Joseph Campbell are: (1973, 3rd Printing) *Hero With a Thousand Faces*. Princeton, New Jersey: Princeton University Press; and, (2001) *Thou Art That: transforming religious metaphor*. Novato, CA: New World Library.

abruptly. If the woman does not examine and manage the jolt to her *psyche*,[2] the resulting intense emotions could become convoluted and develop into self-doubt, victimization, anger, fear and helplessness. She could become anxious, neurotic, depressed, and/or fearful of life. The woman may even become physically ill. Such an emotional complex can significantly affect her life if it is not resolved and objectively put into perspective.

An emotional complex can be defined as an imprint that the human psyche adopts in response to a charged experience. Like a computer, the psyche must store a record of all experiences. The mind's record keeping runs smoothly when experiences meet its expectations of what should transpire. However, emotions, perceptions, and linked events that surround a shock to the psyche are stored as an aggregation of disordered parts. Future situations that the mind associates to one of the entangled fragments may trigger an emotional reaction equal to the initial upheaval.

Emotional psyche shocks do not have to be traumatic or even painful. Pleasant associations, like the euphoria a bride may have experienced during her own beautiful wedding when she felt like a fairy tale princess can also set a subconscious emotional complex into action. In this instance, the woman may become joyful whenever she sees flowers, associating with a happy, dream-come-true celebration. However, the woman may also become illogically disappointed and depressed when her new husband does not choose to give her flowers on our first wedding anniversary.

We often do not know why we feel anxiety, apprehension, fear—or even excitement—in otherwise innocuous situations, but we experience an emotional reaction none-the-less. Emotional residue from psyche shocks is most likely the cause.

In children, even a small upheaval may influence their lives since their tender psyches are easily shocked. Emotional complexes that are set in motion will define their later reactions to life experiences and their beliefs about their world and themselves.

Although the realm of emotions is little understood by many of us, there are a few simple steps for parents to assist their children in developing effective emotional management skills. **The most important step for parents is to**

---

2   The psyche refers to the mind functioning as the center of thought and beliefs that consciously or unconsciously relates the individual to his/her social and physical environment. The psyche also relates to the Soul aspect of an individual.

help their sons and daughters identify and express the emotions they feel.
Children rarely have a grasp of emotions nor have the vocabulary to express
them. The more they practice distinguishing and communicating emotions,
the more proficient and natural at this skill they will become.

Parents who are successful in implementing this crucial step are ones who
know that it is not a sign of weakness when their children feel an emotion.
These parents recognize that emotions are always subjective and individual,
and there is no right or wrong way for their children to feel.

Parents who are sensitive to their children's emotional status will recognize
when their sons or daughters are upset. Some children cry, some strike out,
and some get quiet. In whatever way they express their distress, children are
presenting an opportunity for their parents to ask why they are troubled or
have withdrawn.

For instance, a boy of six may come home from school dejected because
his best friend excluded him in a game. Because it is apparent their son is
distressed, parents can question their son asking, "Did something happen at
school today?" Their son may eventually say, "Richie was mean to me! He
didn't let me play with him!"

The boy's parents can ask him to tell them everything about the situation.
Following the story, they can simply ask, "How does this make you feel?" If
children are young or do not know what the different emotions are, you may
have to suggest and explain emotions to them. For example, "Did this make
you sad? Did this make you angry?" These types of questions not only help
their son become more articulate about emotions, but they also tell him that
it is safe to have emotions and talk about them.

If parents are accepting and non-judgmental, this first step of defining
and expressing specific emotions around a disturbing situation is achieved
more easily. When children have expressed their emotions, the intensity of
the feelings is lessened. Their energy and focus can now be on understanding
the situation and deciding how to proceed, rather than on trying to placate,
dispel or conceal their emotions.

How do parents explain what feelings are to their children? This is an
important question because many of us have not given much thought to
them and how to define even the most basic emotions. We have our own
ideas of what we mean when we say, "I love you," or "That made me angry,"
or "I feel sad." However, if someone were to ask us what we mean, many of
us would have a difficult time explaining exactly how we feel. Children have
an even more difficult time understanding and explaining emotions because
they rarely hear feelings discussed or clearly described. It is therefore a good

idea for parents to equip themselves with some basic definitions that will serve to unify family discussions involving feelings.

Parents can define six basic emotions to children that will assist them immeasurably in understanding the world of subjective feelings. These are *fear*;[3] *joy*;[4] *sadness* or *grief*;[5] *anger*;[6] *pride*;[7] and *shame*.[8] By working with these basic six, parents will have gained experience that further can be applied to more expanded and complex emotions which undoubtedly will surface. The

---

[3]   Fear is an emotion of alarm and agitation caused by the expectation or realization of danger. We feel fear when we do not see ourselves in control in a threatening situation. Several words describe degrees of fear, such as: *Terror; horror; panic; alarm; worry; apprehension; distrust; concern.*

[4]   Joy is an emotion that brings us great pleasure. We feel like we are harmonious with a benevolent and loving world. Words that describe degrees of joy are: *Ecstasy; bliss; delight; enthusiasm; enjoyment; contentment.*

[5]   Sadness and grief are the emotions that describe a mental anguish over a perceived or real loss. We feel that our lives are changed without our approval or decision, or that something that we needed in order to cope with our reality was lost. Words that describe degrees of sadness and grief are: *Inconsolable; despondent; broken-hearted; heartsick; gloomy; melancholic; pitiful; grievous; low-spirited; mournful; "bummed out."*

[6]   Anger is a feeling of extreme displeasure, indignation or exasperation toward someone or something. We often feel anger when we perceive our trust and expectations were exploited. Words that describe degrees of anger are: *Wrath; fury; rage; indignation; resentment; animosity; displeasure; annoyance.*

[7]   Pride is our feeling of self-respect. When someone assumes we are not what we personally think we are, we may feel a shock to our pride, or our sense of self-respect. Words that describe degrees of pride are: *Self-esteem; self-importance; arrogance; haughtiness;" uppitiness"; overconfidence; smugness; self-satisfaction; self-content.*

[8]   Shame is a painful emotion caused by a strong sense of guilt, embarrassment, unworthiness or disgrace. Shame is the most destructive of all emotions if not dealt with, and it is the hardest for children to understand. They may be told that they "should be ashamed of themselves," for something they did. This leads many to think they are dreadful and wicked. When a child acts impulsively or unkindly, a wise parent can help their child understand how to review more appropriate options and assist them in making amends for their reckless or thoughtless actions. When a child believes he should be "ashamed," he carries a heavy life burden. Words that define degrees of shame are: *Mortification; defamation; humiliation; guilt; remorse; embarrassment; disgrace; dishonor; devaluation.*

wider range of words children learn to express themselves and their emotions assists them in them in management of their emotions. It is important that parents, as adults, decide how they will define straightforwardly these six basic emotions for them and their children. All in the family should understand what is meant when any family member uses the words fear, joy, sadness, anger, pride and shame and other words that describe degrees of these six basic emotions.

Children who possess a way to deal with intense feelings are able to make purposeful decisions later in life, despite poignant emotions. Emotionally-savvy individuals put subjective feelings into manageable context.

Emotionally-confident children have resilient *self-esteem*.[9] They are wise because they know that feelings are individual, and that feelings are just feelings. They become more powerful than the emotions they feel, because they consider their feelings and deal with their life situations objectively. In addition to being aware of their own emotions and contending with them, these emotionally-confident children also put into perspective the emotions and judgments of others that are based on emotions. Many individuals judge themselves solely on the basis of how others perceive them and feel toward them. Emotionally-confident children rise above allowing others to define them, and are capable of self-observation and self-determination.

As children grow, the early simple steps to assist them in managing their world of emotions pay far-reaching dividends. **Helping their children recognize and express their feelings in effective language is basic and crucial.** When parents are non-judgmental and allow their sons and daughters to express all feelings, ultimately they will become emotionally confident. Their children will be prepared to meet the world objectively and psychologically, and will be equipped emotionally and intellectually to make essential key life decisions.

The next chapter will discuss decision making, which is the ultimate position of power in self-responsibility.

---

[9]   Genuine self-esteem, valuing and respecting oneself, is based on seeing oneself objectively. How we perceive ourselves often is based on subconscious feelings that frequently have been planted by how others feel about us.

CHAPTER 14

Decision Making

The pinnacle of arriving prepared for adult life is a child's ability to make judicious decisions. Wise decisions are an indicator of intellectual and emotional maturity. A young adult does not miraculously arrive at making insightful choices when he/she reaches 18 or 21. It is a skill that is cultivated throughout his/her youth.

Parents must make many decisions for their sons and daughters in their early years because children lack sufficient knowledge and self-discipline and the capacity of forethought. When parents make decisions that benefit their children's greatest life expressions, their sons and daughters flourish with this wholesome structure and cultivation.

Most children are naturally self-indulgent and self-absorbed. They are learning about themselves and their likes and dislikes. Their early choices will most likely be ones that please the senses and are based on instant gratification. When children receive repeated demonstrations how to make helpful choices regarding themselves they build strong and valuable life-long decision-making habits. It is important to bring a child into the discussion where decisions are considered that relate to them. Perhaps they do not have the final word in the matter, but their input is essential. When the opinions, judgments and feelings of children are respectfully heard, considered and addressed, children are likely to take ownership and commit to the choices made.

How do parents help their children become adept decision-makers? ***Consequences*[1] are the greatest teachers in developing decision-making.** When parents introduce how consequences directly relate to choices, their

---

[1] Consequences are natural results from actions or conditions. There are consequences to every decision and every non-decision.

children establish early the healthy habit of taking responsibility for their decisions and actions. Even an 18-month-old learns not to put fingers in the path of a closing door after a few painful smashes.

To teach their youngsters about consequences, parents can: Remind their children of past similar experiences when they encountered consequences; tell of personal experiences when they, as parents, faced consequences of decisions and actions; share stories that teach consequences; answer questions and offer knowledge needed for wise decision-making.

Children must be kept safe. This requires vigilance when the child's actions might harm him/her or others. However, when children do incur consequences of their conduct, parents later can talk with them about the experience. Review other choices that could have been possible and what consequences these choices could have had. Without judgment, talk about why the child made the decision he/she did. Point out how the decision affected the end result. Use all opportunities to teach about the natural law of cause and effect and point out that all of us learn by looking back on situations and seeing how we might have done things differently.

Opportunities for parents to work with their children in decision-making increase as the youngster(s) get older. Maturing sons and daughters must begin to also make socially-related decisions in addition to physical safety and well-being.

Many teenagers' choices particularly challenge their parents. Unconscious attractions and intense, and frequently un-controlled emotions, often overshadow logic. If a teen was brought up learning to manage emotions and practicing wise decision-making in his/her earlier years, he/she may more quickly assess what social choices might be distressing and unwise for him/her. Oftentimes, however, the only option for parents is to let the child face consequences.

"I told you so," is never appropriate, even when your child made a choice that may not have served his/her best interests. All decisions and their outcomes are learning experiences.

When children are nurtured with acceptance, patience, openness and truthfulness during their formative years, the heart of the decision-making process is in place. If they also receive guidance and assistance in developing healthy management of their emotions, in self-discipline, in determination, in the ability to delay gratification, and in the ability to make commitments to themselves and to follow through on these commitments, the mental components of decision-making is in place. When parents additionally provide appropriate educational and experiential opportunities for their children, the physical elements are also present.

When considering choices and decisions about their children's lives and futures, parents can ask the child, "What feels or seems most like you?" or, "What will serve your greatest good?" These questions, asked routinely, provide their youngsters the knowledge important to consider their developing Authentic Selves. Such questions are significant tools for children to begin to distinguish what choices might best serve them.

Helping children cultivate the skills of decision-making is ongoing for parents. It requires time and patience to repeatedly explain consequences, engage children in discussions about choices, and continually provide necessary information needed to choose wisely. However, when life seems to successfully come together for these young adults, they will be in command of creating their own fulfilling lives. They will not be victims; they will confidently know they control their interactions with life and can face its challenges.

CHAPTER 15

Pulling it All Together

Understanding and working effectively with children comes from parents first gaining *rapport*[1] with their offspring. The effectiveness of the techniques and insights presented in this book depends first on establishing this trusting connection.

To be able to grow and trust him or herself in the world, your child must trust you explicitly. For the child to do this, you must be worthy of that trust. **As your child's first teacher, you are his/her first experience and link with this world. Your impact is enormous.**

In the impressionable early years, it is easy for parents to put off spending the needed time to build a solid foundation with their children. Some assume that the younger the child, the less time is needed in connecting with them. This stems from the opinion that communication is possible only if the child is proficient with the spoken language.

This is a serious misconception. Child psychology research reveals that a very young child who is not adequately stimulated potentially will develop the syndrome of *Failure to Thrive*.[2]

---

[1]   Rapport is mutual trust. To develop mutual trust, one must make a commitment to be honest. For relationships to be a positive, this foundational step is imperative.

[2]   Failure to Thrive in infants and children is usually noticed when they are dramatically smaller or shorter than other children the same age. It is important to determine whether Failure to Thrive results from medical problems with the child or from psycho-social factors in the environment, such as abuse or neglect. There are multiple medical causes of Failure to Thrive that disturb a child's metabolism enough to result in delayed growth. Psychological and social causes

From the perspective of *subtle energetics*[3] what a young child experiences from his immediate family in terms of *energetic resonances*[4] can influence the ease with which talents and potentials develop. When these energetic transmissions are true, honest and pure, the child has much less sorting to do, leaving more energy to be more focused and disciplined.

This may appear time-consuming and a lot of hard work, but this really isn't the case. How much time and energy do you expend when you return the love you feel when your infant holds you captive with his/her bright eyes and smile? Both of you become energized.

The difficulty rests in breaking outdated habits and beliefs. Children and adults have the potential to vibrate a love that embraces and nurtures themselves and others. **Genuine love is an energy that is exponentially powerful, nurturing, and healing. There is no risk involved in the vibration of this love.** A brief moment of this loving exchange is so powerful that it can positively change the course of life.

The movie, ***Pay It Forward,*** is a good example of this love. The child in the movie, in his determination to make a difference in the world, was the instrument of change in the lives of those closest to him. He embodied this love and ultimately broke through his mother's destructive beliefs and habits of reaction. One boy's love, wisdom, acceptance and resoluteness spread, like concentric ripples from the tossing of a pebble in a lake.

Conscious parents are able to help their sons and daughters form strong, positive foundations that, when they are parents, will pass on to their children. As their children's first teachers, parents can teach valuable skills of language and communication, management of emotions, and healthy decision-making. They can plant the seeds of patience, acceptance, openness

---

may include emotional deprivation as a result of parental withdrawal, rejection, or hostility. Economic factors can affect living conditions, nutrition and parental attitudes. Risk factors for Failure to Thrive are related to the causes and may include undiagnosed diseases, negative emotional environments, poverty, and crowded or unsanitary living conditions.

3   Subtle energetics is the subtle states of being, such as thought, belief, and emotion which create our physical reality.

4   Anytime a person feels an emotion, either negative or positive, there is an emotional energetic resonance held in his/her energy field. Those who are sensitive to these resonances can be easily influenced by them. For instance, sensitive people are happier in the company of happy people. They will tend to be more depressed in the company of depressed people.

and truthfulness. These ideals can bear remarkable fruit throughout their children's lifetimes.

Children blessed with conscious parents will impact their world. They will love and be loved, and each will influence the world and humanity. Children who have learned and experienced the simple fundamentals outlined in this book become secure and confident. They possess tools to maintain balance and centeredness.

Children are truly the hope for the future. Let us help free and empower them to live the brilliant and creative lives they are meant to live.

SAMPLE QUESTIONS AND ANSWERS

Based on actual experiences, the following questions and answers may be helpful to parents . . . .

* * *

Our 4-year-old son has always been very quiet and somewhat withdrawn. He is our only child. Our son rarely wants to play with other children, and is most content when engaged in an individual activity like playing with building blocks and computer games. He is so unlike other children I know, and I am concerned that he doesn't seem to mix with other children. What do you suggest?

We must look past the idea of a "normal" child. Instead, we need to distinguish if your son is naturally introspective or if he is withdrawing out of depression, anxiety or fear. If he has always been focused, quiet and reserved, being introspective is probably his nature.

Begin to include him in play groups for short periods of time, allowing him to be around other children. This will help to develop his social interaction skills. Carefully choose the parents and children. Make sure that when you are not supervising your son's play group, you get honest feedback from other parents about your son's interaction with other children.

You can be of great service to your son by gently teaching him helpful behaviors and manners, such as sharing and being helpful, which will lessen the social distance between him and others. It is important that you also remind him that being kind is always a wise thing to do. A child can understand kindness as sharing a smile, including others in play, and helping another in need. By guiding him in matters of the heart (acceptance, compassion, honesty, and openness) he begins to learn that these help his relationships.

If you find that your son is uncomfortable in a group, it is important that you allow him to be himself while involved in the interaction. A child will often work out a group dynamic if left to his own devices. We adults, however, tend to want to direct the play of children before giving them a chance to work through a conflict. By watching your child within a group, you will learn a great deal about him and his gifts and challenges.

After the play period is over, engage your son in a conversation by asking him questions. "What did you like best about playing with the group today?" Or, "What did you like least about playing with the group today?" "If you could change anything about this day, what would it be?" These questions allow your son to clarify his feelings and build his inner glossary and vocabulary. Your non-judgmental questions also help him communicate with you, so that as his parent, you gain valuable understanding into the uniqueness of your child. When you know what he is thinking and feeling, it is much easier to encourage and assist him.

Naturally quiet children tend to be observant and logical. If this description fits your child, it is wise to provide him with toys and tools that will further develop his intrinsic abilities. At the same time, you can also help him develop social interaction skills that he may lack.

It is most important that he knows you accept him just the way he is. If championed for his uniqueness at home, he will grow to like himself and will more easily find his own way.

*   *   *

My wife and I do not agree on discipline for our two daughters (ages 8 and 10). I think my wife is far too lenient because she allows them to tear up the house and talk back to us. My wife gets angry when I tell our daughters to clean up their messes and to treat us with respect and thinks I am too strict and non-caring.

It may be that your daughters are confused because they have observed two very different parenting styles. They may also feel caught in the middle of your arguments. Over time, they get frustrated, and the only way your daughters may know how to express their confusion is by disruptive behavior. Their conduct, in turn, can widen the division among the family members.

I would suggest that you read *Chapter 5* of this book that deals with parenting styles. Do the overly-permissive and overly-authoritarian styles apply to you and your wife? I would suggest that you and your wife talk truthfully about what might be going between the two of you. Are your daughters causing your quarrels, or are they the scapegoats? In other words, are there other issues between you and your wife that may be the cause of your disagreements? Children are intuitive but rarely have the words to express what they are sensing. Another alternative for you is to attend a parenting class. Many parents have found them valuable.

When you and your wife reach a point where you agree to cooperate for the benefit of your children, involve the entire family in a discussion. You might begin by saying, "We have a problem in our family, and that problem is causing us adults to fight and you children to be confused. We think it might center round our differences in what we believe to be important to be as parents. What do you think?"

Even though they may not say much at the first meeting, pre-adolescent children usually sigh in relief when they can speak their truth. Finding the truth of a matter is the quickest way to solving a problem. No one wants a disharmonious family, least of all children.

When parents are open to working out a solution to benefit everyone, they are modeling cooperation, acceptance and teamwork to their children. The whole family benefits greatly!

* * *

Our 3-year-old daughter has talked about three unexpected deaths before they have happened. What is going on with her, and how can we best help her?

As was discussed previously, children can be *very* intuitive. Your daughter seems to be intuitive. As with any talent or potential in a child, it is important to withhold judgment. If you believe that each child is unique this will help her integrate her atypical skills.

Your daughter pre-recognizes the dying of others. This may seem macabre. However, children do not attach morose feelings to a death/dying process. It is quite possible that your daughter perceives an energy field around those who are preparing to leave the body. Death is not of great concern because it is a natural occurrence to her.

You can be of great help to your daughter by being compassionate, helping her to understand her talents, and assisting her to put her uncommon abilities into perspective. Others can be attracted to people with uncommon talents or may be wary of them. It is important for your daughter to know that, as she begins to develop her potentials and introduces them into the world, she always has supportive parents.

No matter what innate abilities and qualities your child is born with, let her know that your gifts to her will be patience, acceptance, openness and truthfulness.

*   *   *

My 7-year-old son is hyperactive and is having a difficult time settling down in school. I receive notes from his teacher that he is disruptive to the class, and the teacher suggests that I work with him at home. The problem is that I have absolutely no idea how to do this. We yell at him and ground him to try to impress on him that he needs to pay attention, but nothing works.

Instead of punishing their children for something that they are having difficulty doing, I suggest to parents to try other measures. First talk with your son and listen to his side of the difficulty. If he can't express himself, suggest a few hypothetical reasons for what is happening. Ask if he thinks he has a difficult time keeping his mind on what he is doing. Ask if he would rather play or talk to others than do the work. Occasionally a 7-year-old is homesick, and he causes diversions in order not to think about his longing for home. There can be other reasons for your son's disruptiveness at school, and your job as a parent is to try to uncover his reason.

You are wise to include your child in the solution process by asking him to partner with you in solving the problem and overcoming his challenge. I guarantee that your child wants the situation resolved as much as everyone else does. When he is included, your son will assume responsibility for himself and gain valuable experience in finding creative solutions to his problems. He will also receive validation that he is a force in his own life.

If there is a silver lining here, it is that you are beginning to work with him early in his school experience. Oftentimes these types of problems are ignored or treated as behavioral problems for several years. When this happens, emotional and mental scars form, adding to the child's difficulties.

A few considerations that may help in approaching your son's current difficulties are:

1. He may learn differently than how his teacher commonly teaches. Possibly your son learns by doing rather than by listening or seeing.

Perhaps you can solicit the teacher's help to present the material in an additional way. You, as a parent, can always work with your son at home in this manner. A former teacher reminded me that from her point of view, it is imperative that the teacher and parent conference on the child's difficulties and behavior. Otherwise, assumptions are made on both sides, and often little progress is made.

2. Maybe school is just uninteresting. This is common with a child who is intelligent beyond his years. Such a child can lose interest in rote learning. If this is the case, attaching basic learning, such as reading or math skills to the study of his interests may help. Often we must use creative ways to confront the learning dilemmas of such a child. I was one of these children. I learned but rarely reached what authorities considered my potential. I was much too fearful to be outwardly hyperactive, but my mind was always jumping from one thing to another. In college, life began for me when I took my first psychology course. Rarely reading until that time, I then read voraciously because I was interested in what I was reading! Other subjects also became important because they were related to, and would help me master, what I came to study and do in this world.

3. Help your son to center and focus. Engage him in pretending that he is a tree. (It is important that he is not forced to stand as a tree for longer periods that he is able to handle. 10 seconds to a child is like 10 minutes to an adult.) For children, making practice or learning exercises fun is valuable, and most children love company! Perhaps you can watch and time your son for 10 seconds, and then he can watch and time you for a specified time. In that way, he is concentrating both as a tree, and as an observer of you being a tree. Make sure he knows the rules; trees stand absolutely still! He can then make sure you know the rules! As I discussed in Chapter 12, *Family Decrees*, remind your son often to take a deep breath to help him center and focus. (An initial deep breath could be included in the rules.) Increase the time of this focusing exercise when he is ready. This child meditation has other psycho-spiritual benefits, but it is particularly helpful for those who have attention challenges.

4. If your son continues to be disruptive and inattentive, ask your school counselor or other school representative for a list of area resources that dedicate themselves to attention problems. Be vigilant about whom you choose! Make sure he/she is working with your child for his benefit. Some focus on solving the school's and the teacher's problems

only. One of my teachers once said, "There are no problems, only challenges to overcome!" If you are intent upon helping your child, sooner or later a solution will be found.

*   *   *

My 32-year-old daughter was killed recently in an automobile accident and our family is devastated. She left behind her 5-year-old daughter. She and her mother were very close, and we have no idea what to do for her or what to say to her.

It is worth mentioning that in situations like this, children are not only dealing with the loss of their parent, but they are also dealing with the grieving of other family members and a profound change in their lives. A young child rarely has the vocabulary or acumen to ask questions she needs answered in order to begin to put her life back on track.

It is crucial to give your granddaughter a compassionate, but truthful, explanation about her mother's death. Also ask frequently if she has any questions. It is also helpful to talk about her mom and things you remember and loved about your daughter. This will show your granddaughter it is okay to talk about her mother and the times she shared with her.

Young children perceive events as an extension of themselves, and it is very easy for them to record their loss as resulting from something they are, said or did. This misconception often is reinforced because no one clarifies the assumption. Reassure the child that she was in no way responsible for her mother's death. Questions and honesty will also encourage your granddaughter to talk to you about her feelings and help her grasp of the circumstances.

Secondly, know that she is witnessing your deep sadness and is trying to make sense of that. It will be helpful to explain to her that death is a part of living and that sometimes we don't understand why someone leaves early in life. (But make clear to her that she had nothing to do with the accident or the death of her mother.) It is also important for her to know that although things are and will be different, she will always have people who care for her and who will be there for her.

I believe it is important to seek the services of a grief specialist who works with children. Adults in the family usually have very little time and energy for the special needs of a small child because of their own grieving process. Capable grief professionals can tremendously help a child with loss and the grieving process.

GLOSSARY

Acceptance—Unconditionally believing that, "Whatever is happening or presenting in the moment is most appropriate." It is equally important to consider that whatever we are feeling or being in the moment is largely a result of our conditioning and is also appropriate. When we accept unconditionally and do not judge our feelings, our realities or our thoughts (and those of others) as good/bad or right/wrong, we allow ourselves to assume the wise and empowering position of the observer. As observer, the opportunity is present to make discerning observations concerning the truthfulness of our assumptions and our beliefs. Equally empowering is the fact that we then give ourselves a choice as to how we respond to what is happening in that moment, rather than unconsciously reacting out of habit.

Adult (healthy)—A being incarnate who has mastered skills and knowledge to a sufficient degree to interact successfully with his/her physical and social environment.

Anger—Anger is a feeling of extreme displeasure, indignation or exasperation toward someone or something. We often feel anger when we perceive our trust and expectations were exploited. Words that describe degrees of anger are: *Wrath, fury; rage; indignation; resentment; animosity; displeasure; annoyance.*

Authentic Self—The Self that seeks joyful and genuine expression through physical life. It has been defined by some as the "Soul," and by others as the "Higher Self or God Self." The energy of this Self animates and brings life to the physical body. Some view this Self as not being able to express fully through our physical forms because of the hold and control that the ego (the lower self) has been able to assume. The Authentic Self cannot be present when a negative environment has been created, which is the type of environment on which the ego thrives.

Campbell, Joseph—Joseph Campbell (1904-1987) was an author and lifelong student and professor of the human spirit and comparative mythology. *(See footnote Chapter 13.)*

Character and Body Costume—An individual's character and body costume is one's physical expression at any given time. We often believe that this expression, the one we know in this lifetime, is the only one we ever had. Our essence, however, has had many characters and bodies throughout its evolution. It is quite likely it will have many more.

Child (healthy psycho-spiritually)—A being incarnate who has not yet mastered the potential skills and knowledge necessary to successfully inhabit his/her physical and social environment.

Commitment—Commitment is a pledge to keep an agreement or accomplish a course of action successfully. A commitment is an agreement you make to yourself, but does not necessarily benefit others. It is important to understand what one can be responsible for in terms of making a commitment. For instance, if one makes the commitment to make another happy, this is not a realistic commitment. One does not (and cannot) possess the power to make another happy. One can create diversion in another's life that for a time will supersede or overshadow unhappiness, but one's happiness is one's own responsibility.

Communication Package—The collective ways we communicate our thoughts, emotions and our state of energetic balance outwardly, both subtly and in more commonly recognizable ways. Humanity relies heavily upon the spoken word in its communication. Words are extremely powerful and can be quite helpful. However, they can also become a tool to deceive or control others. Those who are intuitive (and many children are before they are taught to discredit this profound tool) are distinguishing and reacting to the state of the energetic field. When we are able to interpret the energy field correctly, we enter into the clearest form of communication.

Compassion—Profound respect and honor for another's journey.

Composure—Composure denotes self-awareness, self-possession, self-reliance and calmness, even in the face of distractions and excitable situations.

Concept—A concept is a general understanding of something.

Confidence—Throughout this book, confidence refers to *". . . the expression of your essential, authentic, primal self . . . [the inner state of mind] that you are capable and lovable."* Quote from the teachings of Jerhoam, an enlightened consciousness teacher. (More information may be obtained through website *www.Jerhoam.com*.) You express confidence when you express who you innately are.

Conditional Love (*Conditional Acceptance*)—Conditional love is more a conditioning tool than an emotion. It is based on the concept that, "I will love you if you please me." Conditional love is the prime reason we have lost our direction in matters of the heart. The resonation of "love" automatically triggers the opening of the heart center, but conditional love has little to do with the heart. It is manipulative and is a mind game.

Consequences—Consequences are natural results from actions or conditions. There are consequences to every decision and every non-decision.

Creativity—Creativity is the ability to think "outside the box." It is the foundation of original thought, invention and problem-solving.

Destiny—The assumption is made in this writing that each of us has an individual evolutionary agenda that our Soul, or Authentic Self, has defined to complete or gain in accomplishment with regard to the current lifetime. There is great joy and anticipation when we discover our destiny and begin to focus on its actualization.

Drama—Drama refers to the soap opera reality we usually find ourselves in when we participate in negative emotional games. These games involve the negative type of emotions such as judgment, greed, lust, fear, hate, jealousy, control, revenge, competition, etc.

Elixir—An elixir, metaphorically, refers to a magical type of element or agent that changes negativity into positivism. In alchemy, an elixir is often thought of as a magical or medicinal potion that transforms base metals into gold. Spiritually, it has been referred to as a magical agent that offers eternal or everlasting life.

Emotional Makeup—Our emotional makeup pertains to how we have interpreted our life to the present moment. This history plays a large part in how we will interpret and be affected by our lives both now and in the future.

Emotions—Emotions are complex and sometimes strong subjective responses. When feeling a strong emotional reaction, physiologic changes actually occur that prepare the individual who is feeling the strong emotion for physical action. Strong emotions result when something happens or someone does something that is unexpected.

Energetic Resonances—Anytime a person feels an emotion, either negative or positive, there is an emotional energetic resonance held in his/her subtle body. Those who are sensitive to these resonances can easily be influenced by them. For instance, sensitive people are happier in the company of happy people. They will tend to be more depressed in the company of depressed people.

Energy Dynamics—Energy dynamics is energy movement and flow and its resulting effects and transformations.

Essential (Essence)—The essence of something or someone is its unchanging, intrinsic nature in its most pure form.

Evolutionary History—Evolutionary history is based upon the belief that the Soul is currently utilizing several lifetimes to complete its process to return to The Oneness with God, The Creator, The One, The Universe, The All That Is, or whatever title an individual prefers. The experiences, wisdom and knowledge garnered to this end make up the Soul's evolutionary history.

Failure to Thrive—(See footnote Chapter 15.)

Fear—Fear is an emotion of alarm and agitation caused by the expectation or realization of danger. We feel fear when we do not see ourselves in control in a threatening situation. Several words describe degrees of fear, such as: *Terror; horror; panic; alarm; worry; apprehension; distrust; concern.*

Feelings—Feelings are emotional responses that cause us to react. This reaction can be positive, opening the heart to vibrate with joy and happiness. The reaction can also be negative, causing our hearts to close and protect itself. This prompts us to be defensive, attacking or controlling.

Glossary—A listing of words and an explanation of their specialized meanings that allow a deeper understanding of subtle concepts presented in a body of text.

Good Karma—Good Karma results when both the giver and the receiver benefit from an act of good will. Simply put, good karma is the dynamic that exemplifies the old saying, "You reap what you sow." It illustrates the principle of cause and effect.

Impeccability—Impeccable means flawless. In our context, it means using precise and exact words, which truthfully and clearly express both thoughts and feelings.

Intuitive—One who is sensitive to, and can interpret, energetic communications.

Joy—Joy is an emotion that brings us great pleasure. We feel like we are harmonious with a benevolent and loving world. Words that describe degrees of joy are: Ecstasy; bliss; delight; enthusiasm, enjoyment; contentment.

Judgment(al)—A tool of discerning thought that, when used in a negative way, automatically sets up moralistic thought and separative dynamics. This happens when one thinks in terms of good or bad, right or wrong, righteous or sinner, better than or worse than. Authentic compassion cannot coexist in a mind that is critically judgmental.

Life Mission—Our life mission refers the collective of what we are to experience, accomplish and learn in order for our Soul to grow and evolve.

Love—Love has many meanings, and while most are highly charged emotionally, many of them carry a lot of negative baggage, i.e., emotional addictions. Addictions are more accurately defined in terms of "attachment" rather than "love." However, when one is experiencing a high vibration of love, there is nothing like it. In that moment, the person feels at one with everything; the energetic connection is profound, and negativity is nonexistent. Because we are in a physical dimension, we often experience gradients of this high vibrational emotion and our hearts open to share without expecting reciprocity.

Mind—The mind is the imperceptible component of our being that accumulates assumed facts, memories and beliefs about ourselves, others and our environments. It is the component that is frequently thought of as our consciousness and the faculty of thinking, reasoning and applying knowledge. The mind's physical instrument is the brain.

Mind Patterns—Mind patterns are powerful patterns of beliefs and thoughts that create our reactions and our life experiences. For instance, if we are naturally happy and believe we will be fortunate in life, that mind pattern will manifest itself. On the other hand, if we believe that we are always being slighted, that mind pattern will also manifest itself.

Parental Style—A parenting style is a parent's most consistent way of responding or reacting toward his/her child.

Patience—The ability to understand and to work harmoniously with natural law and natural cycles.

Perfect Child—A perfect child is one that meets criteria that he/she must meet to rank in a system of power and hierarchy. There is no such child who is perfect, although some parents strive unsuccessfully and blindly to create one. This especially happens to a first-born.

Potential—The collective and unique individual capacities and innate qualities we are born with. Potentials are key elements in the unfoldment of our destinies and in our ongoing spiritual evolution.

Power—The application of wisdom, knowledge and talents. When power is in balance, it is used to benefit all living things involved.

Pride—Pride is our feeling of self-respect. When someone assumes we are not what we personally think we are, we may feel a shock to our pride, or our sense of self-respect. Words that describe degrees of pride are: *Self-*

esteem; self-importance; arrogance; haughtiness; "uppitiness"; overconfidence; smugness; self-satisfaction; self-content.

Psyche—The psyche refers to the mind functioning as the center of thoughts and beliefs that consciously or unconsciously relate the individual to his/her social and physical environment. The psyche also relates to the Soul aspect of an individual.

Psycho-spiritual—A model of thought and theory that concentrates upon the connection of feelings and emotions as a link to the Spiritual or Higher Self. In this model of thought, feelings are utilized as a tool to help uncover the blocks and misconceptions of truth that keep us from realizing our *Authentic Self* and our most glorious expression possible.

Rapport—Rapport is mutual trust. To develop mutual trust, one must make a commitment to be honest. For relationships to be positive, this foundational step is imperative.

Reincarnation—There are many forms of belief regarding reincarnation, but a basic and fundamental principle underlying various philosophies and schools is this (as paraphrased from W. W. Atkinson, *Reincarnation and The Law of Karma*; Yogi Publication Society; 1936: p.8): That there is, in man, an "immaterial *Something*" called Soul, Spirit, Inner Self, etc., which does not perish at the death or disintegration of the body, but that continues as an entity. This entity, after an interval of rest and possible reflection, is re-born into a new infant body and proceeds to live a new life in the new body, more or less unconscious of its past existences. Even though largely unconscious of past life experiences, the being contains within itself the "essence" or results of its past lives. These past experiences play an important role in determining its new character or personality.

Sadness—Sadness and grief are the emotions that describe a mental anguish over a perceived or real loss. We feel that our lives are changed without our approval or decision, or that something that we needed in order to cope or be happy with our reality was lost. Words that describe degrees of sadness and grief are: *Inconsolable; despondent; broken-hearted; heartsick; gloomy; melancholic; pitiful; grievous; low-spirited; mournful; "bummed out."*

Seed—A belief or thought form that is usually held in the mind as an assumption of truth. When a seed is accepted as truth and diligently tended to, it grows and becomes a fundamental belief that governs our sense of reality. If these seeds are not rooted in absolute truth, however, they cause dissonance in our lives and block the experience of our Authentic Selves and authentic reality.

Self-esteem, genuine—Genuine self-esteem, valuing and respecting oneself, results from seeing oneself objectively. How we perceive ourselves often is based on subconscious feelings that frequently have been planted by how others feel about us.

Shame—Shame is a painful emotion caused by a strong sense of guilt, embarrassment, unworthiness or disgrace. Shame is the most destructive of all emotions if not dealt with, and it is the hardest for children to understand. Perhaps they are often told that they "should be ashamed of themselves," for something they did. This leads many to think they are dreadful and wicked. When a child acts impulsively or unkindly, a wise parent can help their son or daughter understand how to review more appropriate options and assist them in making amends for their reckless or thoughtless actions. When a child believes he should be "ashamed," he carries a heavy life burden. Words that define degrees of shame are: *Mortification; defamation; humiliation; guilt; remorse; embarrassment; disgrace; dishonor; devaluation.*

Spiritual Identity—Our spiritual identity is who we are innately. It refers to the unique individuality of our Soul.

Subconscious—The part of the mind that contains assumptions, data and programming which one is not fully aware of, but that has a profound controlling influence upon actions and feelings.

Subtle—That which is not easily perceived with the physical senses of touch, taste, sight, hearing and smell. Even though we are not usually consciously aware of the world and reality of the *subtle*, it is this reality that creates our world of the obvious.

Subtle Energetics—Refers to the subtle states of being, such as thought, belief and emotion which create our physical reality.

True—When I use the word *true* by itself or as the root of another, I am referring to that which conforms in essence with the natural or universal laws. I believe that when we speak in such phrases as, "My truth is . . ." or, "That is your truth . . ." when we actually mean, "I believe that . . ." we corrode the pure meaning of the word.

Unconditional Love—As closely as we can understand it, unconditional love is total acceptance of whatever has emerged without judgment or urge to necessarily fix it or dispose of it.

Unconscious—That part of the mind that holds the data, programming and other encoding that is relevant to our overall spiritual evolutional process and unfoldment. This is perhaps the least obvious of the world of subtle energetics because it is almost inaccessible to the conscious mind. The data that is held in the unconscious greatly influences the inherited conditions of life, our beliefs, our behavior and our emotions, respectively.

Victim—A victim is a role that is assumed by individuals when they do not know their power to change a negative situation. For them, someone or something else is responsible for whatever unpleasantness they feel.

Vulnerability—Vulnerability is the state of being in total trust. This state of being is extremely threatening to our personalities and our egos, but when subtle energetics is profoundly understood, there is an absolute knowledge that great power is inherent in any moment we represent ourselves authentically.